Sunspot Literary Journal

2022

Creativity is Power

Sunspot Literary Journal 2022
Volume 4 Issue 4
Creativity is power

Published by Sun Dogs Creations
Changing the World One Book at a Time
Print ISBN: 978-1-951389-27-7
eBook ISBN: 978-1-951389-28-4

Cover Image *Tranquil Forest Tiger (Summer)* by Roopa Dudley
Cover Design by Angel Leya
Sunspot Logo by Timothy Boardman

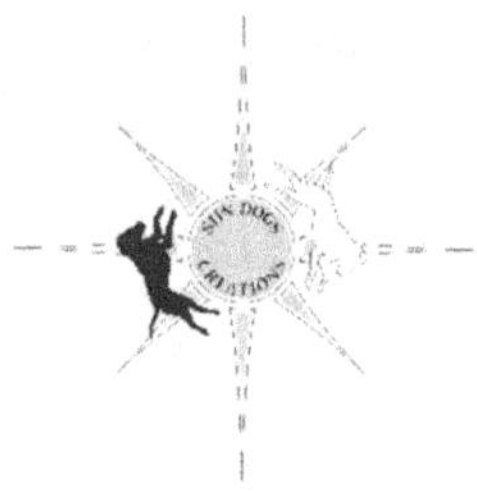

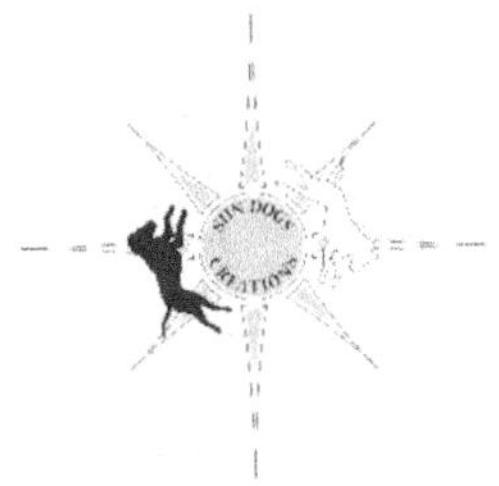

Table of Contents

Inception 2021

Culmination 2021

Geminga 2022

Rigel 2022

[LA BODA LA MUERTE MI VIDA]

Adam Walsh

Editor's Prize

Sometime after light bleached our faces to a photo
          not the studio kind   thick gloss   opaque background
polaroid even   not enough context for the story
repeated to strangers at a passthrough bar near stateline
with a common unmemorable name
brought out any chance to say: *esta foto   es mi chica*
ella siempre está conmigo   kept in wallet to stay
too long   and me   sitting on it   if that's not...

          huh?   how did it happen?   when did it end?

in '81 *cuando la vida dejo de servir los frutos del trabajo*
fields fat to founder   *rojo   verde*   rotten   *dulce*

          where'd you go then?   ¡¿a dónde?!

con mi foto   con mi cerverza   with a short book of songs
                    yo estoy aquí   walking *el campo negro*
blackenedfeet kicking up the soft ash from my reckoning

          then why...why are you here?

that   i can't tell you my friend   not yet anyway
maybe after this pint   or a different day altogether
when the pages of this book   *canciones y todo*
          no longer need to be sung
only quiet remains   except for   *lluvia*
                    sí   lluvia   i'll certainly tell you the next time
          we come in from the rain

Waiting for the Commands

Jose Varghese

It begins in the year of extinctions. The breeze that used to
lick off sweat from the back of your neck
in summer days is gone. You hide behind the hefty ceramic
pickle jars, solaced by its cold, glossy exterior.
The aroma of whole ripe mangoes that're preserved in them
with salt, oil and dry red chilies, seeps through
the cloth that's tied tight over its lid with several strands
of jute. No one has told you about the absences
you were to be made with, in a world that's not yet ready
for your cultivated skills of flawless accumulation
of data and accurate response to commands, gained more
from machines than humans. You still imagine
yourself to be a part of them, but those races and genders
and faiths confuse you as much as the pickles
they make, the ideologies they use to fight with one another,
the green and red and blue caps they sport
to show how they differ from one another, the snacks and
drinks and words they choose to declare
their love or hurt or hatred at night, in dimly-lit terraces
with yellow walls. You were born out of their
collective ambition, but no one accepts you for what you've
become in their hands. You still dream of the hills
on all sides cradling the home that you thought was yours.
The smell of jackfruit and guava, the squeaky
squirrels that hung upside-down from plantains, the frantic
movement of their tails and cacophonous praise

of the cornucopia they thought of as theirs while they ate
and drank to their fill in dimly-lit dusks
with amber skies, the parakeets playing hide-and-seek with
gooseberry leaves, the snakes coiling around
the dried-up secrets of the sun, the pheromone-driven
processions of the ants—are all in the past, as
you wait for commands from radio hisses and rumbles,
hiding behind the last mangoes in pickle jars.

The Red Sea

Bianca Giglio

i.

there is sea water everywhere

it's in my memories
in my nightmares
it's streaming down the road
carrying flowers with it
and sashes that read *our deepest condolences*

it's carrying her butchered body
out to the ocean
and everyone can see her heart
but no one can see her hands

her hands—the butcher
her body—the lamb
her heart—just another dried field
just another abandoned building

ii.

sorry about the mess

that's what her next of kin told me

when there were boxes everywhere
when they were just trying to find a home
someplace more than temporary
someplace that smelled like them again

as it so happens, that's just what i've been
trying to find a way to tell them all this time
without making them relive everything:
i'm sorry about the mess
i'm sorry the couch was white
i'm sorry we didn't scrub harder
i'm sorry about the blankets, the pillows, the missing remote
i'm sorry if you could still see the stains
the yellow spots where you know blood used to be

really, there's only so much a spray bottle
and a roll of paper towels can do—
this i know theoretically

the enormity of the red sea is too great
and the pain ran deeper than the blood anyway

iii.

mary, mary

sea and rosary

how does your garden grow?

with lampwork beads

and apple seeds

and the graves all in a row

HOW RADIANT, HOW FEARFUL TO BEHOLD

KATE STRONG STADT

To see the glory of the face
of my childhood God

is to blister and pant,
wax wings in ascent.

To land,
a man.

Cruising is Such a Drag / Tyler McCurry

In This World Love

JJ Chen Henderson

In this world, love
is undefinable.
Easier to just say it is
a look.
An hour.
A phone call.
A kidney.
Bone marrow.

In this world, love
is overrated.
She longs
for the song
he hums
each time
he rolls over.

In this world, love
may not even look like
love. How else
do you explain
his habit
of lifting her
as weight?

In this world, love
has no analogy.
But why,
as I break off
a rhizome
of lotus root,
in its many lake-mud-
smeared hollows,
I see the blanks
in my aging mother's
eyes?

In this world, love
comes with
a price. This grief
makes me
doubt
if I should've loved
my father without ever
bargaining.

There Was the Spotted Pony

Murray Silverstein

There was the spotted pony, bells on its harness, the old man led to our door.
Lifting me onto the saddle, he put a black sombrero on my head, a kerchief
round my neck, and snapped a picture he sold to my mother, whose mother
was crushed by a horse-drawn wagon on the family farm.

Who can say what it is to be alive on this earth? Not me.

There was Riley, near-blind and living alone across the court, fish tank
by his door, the tank so full of plants and slime, I couldn't see the fish.
They're there, claimed Riley, *keep looking*, and gave me a book on fishing,
the word *angler* fresh to my eyes: to read, to watch, to wait.

You'd think, giving us eyes, it's begging to be seen, this world, to be known.

And there was my father, washing our car on the street, saying, *Go in & get me a beer.*
Filled with meaning I hop on my trike, and bumping along on its crooked wheels
shake the can of Schlitz, and it explodes all over the car. Father, whose father fled

the burning *shtetl*, throwing down his chamois cloth, cursing me, my trike and the beer.

Born into time, believing it's ours, our time, until, open to pain and desire,
I *am the author of time*, says the earth, *and you belong to me.*

But wait, my sister's nightstand, in the room we shared, her ice skates beneath it
in a leather zippered *Polar Palace* bag, where, when she left it open, you could see
the flashing blades!

Everything seen is ruled by the sun, whose law you learn by heart:
Who tries to look straight at me will go blind.

No. Shout it, there *WAS* . . . across Third Street, a field, unfenced, Gilmore's,
where Ringling Brothers pitched its tents, saw the bearded lady, Lottie Letz,
while a dozen horse-head oil rigs churned the deep, turning a fractured *is*
into the idyll *was*—can hear them still in my sleep.

You were given a life, consciousness, dreams, a mother-tongue
with which to praise—all of what is, was, and is
beyond your power to say.

Another Dream About Death

Ryan Mattern

The water here is all surface,
shallow as this paper.
Its depths drown nothing.

To swim is to long,
to freeze is to wait.

The waves unfurl onto a plyboard
shore. The oblong moon,
furious in new light,
yanks the tide from my feet.

The men hunting abalone
walk bentbacked and aching,
their buckets dragging behind them.

A shorebird circles
the same carve of bay

drawn by string,
its poor watered wings.
I don't know for how long
a thing can be weary.

Melting Demon Gravel Pit

/ Christopher Paul Brown

Dream of Emma Returning

Alex Stanley

All of my logic points to coincidence,
unless dreams are like roots in a forest,
connecting everything. I dreamt of you
the night your father died, made a note of it,
that you returned to me, that you were happy.
It's been three years since we last spoke,
yet I heard you cry, thousands of miles away,
waking me in my sleep, here, beyond the confines
of love, arms, the smoothing of your eyelids,
and when you told me you'd never speak to me
again, I didn't know another world could open.

Ergo Age

Alex Stanley

I walk in the spring that light warmth brings—
I walk in the sky that rages from night into day
as the bright ocean breeze grows silent as gold.
Let's leave the Appalachians and travel past
the Missouri into the glow of harvest wheat—
we will walk clear to the Pacific if we have to.
I walk with an impatient mind longing to wander.
I walk with a joyful spirit—my feet grow callused.
My charming friend, our encounter is fulfilled
down the road, at a time when we will make a home
out of our different paths, each leading back to the other.[1]

[1] *Ergo Age* is a translation of Catullus's *Carmen XLVI.*

Chess-Nut Forest (Autumn)

/ Roopa Dudley

Frigid Forest Fox (Winter)

/ Roopa Dudley

Chess-Nut Paradise (Spring)

/ Roopa Dudley

CHESS-NUT SWAMP / ROOPA DUDLEY

Pick Me a Color

Travis Stephens

"Help me pick a nail color,"

she said
standing before a display of
lozenges, of glossy oval
plastic tongues &
racks of tiny bottles.
Pick the color of shred,
pick the color of heartbreak,
the exact shade of laughter
in an overheated room.
Not the color of overheard
conversations
with other girlfriends,
of casual embraces &
long goodbyes.
Try the shade of despair
or a reeling sense of shame.
Dab the laugh at own's expense,
the faded shoes gone musty
& too small.
The way a shared sweater fits best,
never jeans, maybe jacket.
Pick a color that says
only me

not Lisa or Lizette, a teacher
the parents or
God forbid, a boy.
Pick me a color of want.

“Pink,” I said,
“pink is nice.”

My Wife Dies During Birth

Oisin Farraige

1.

Spinal tap then split her stomach open in
front of me. chiral winged death. angel
of the other side looming, crying in

want. crossing over provides certain
particulars for the attentive soldier of
god. the frontline is you, in the maternity

ward. the bridge is the depth of will
to cross it. this soul economy has
taken its toll and crossed you. though

you've taken your last you've given new.

2.

new blood it would've been in my time,
my son. there's this bending of the air
around you, heat death of father bonds.

i can't help but pile blame upon you,
lump flesh of mine, take and take is all
you seem to do. then you grasp at that

air and it insulates you, by the time you're
in my arms I've taken responsibility. little
glimmers of her brighten your crib: your

eyes and the patterned walls and sheets,
mobiles, toys she took ages searching for
into near perfect matches for the bump.

you sprang up faster than I could have
imagined, into something far greater than
your parts. maybe more of her was taken

for how unlike myself it seems you are.

After My Wife's Funeral

Oisin Farriage

//

I wrote down
Everything
That I felt

Struck light
Out of dark
To burn these poems

Thinking If I could rid earth
Of every
Trace
I
Could let her go . . .

Now I spend the rest
Of my life
Writing to keep her here

//

Color, scent, voice, touch of hand,
heart, driven out by time—
Straws if ever grasped again— always trying
In a sushi restaurant seated for one.

My Grandfather Tells Me His Story in a Dream After His Death

Oisin Farriage

In the hills of Kentucky, where old men sit and
read small town papers   Where tossed bike
frames crawl the walk in front of Bennet's,
tripping men for Ale-8 sips   Where a plow is
pushed by cracked hands against impotent sod
Where the gravestone of my grandfather lies
disturbed, footpaths unbeaten Where the
mountaintop has been blown to pieces—soaked
the hollers in sickness for cars and comfort   Where
you get sun at ten—lose it at two   Where as
young as six you can tote your father's dynamite
for him   You can haul a coal bucket one
hundred feet deep   You can watch him clutch
his chest at your eighth birthday party searching
for breath   You can see your own future—hacked
black globs filtered through bleeding lungs—in
the toilet bowl after one of his *fits*   You can see
his pale face before they close the lid   You can
watch your mother open the only mail from the
coal company to no letter and a check for half of
his weekly pay   You can stop for gas thirty
years later at a Circle K and suffocate on your
phlegm going to take a piss in the bathroom
while your grandson pumps gas

Hair

Candice Kelsey

I like the moments when my hair is almost dry / wading away from damp / the lingering between private / & public self / between familiar, naked, wet / a body / & unfamiliar, clothed, dry / a shape entering the world / like a yawn / or the evidence of birth / each of us once a newborn swathed in womb-remnants / wet / no stopping the nurse from toweling our head. / Why are we so quick to rid ourselves of life / of the signs of struggle / that first quest for light / to find breath's rhythm? / Today the sun dries my hair / doing what it does / every day / we rarely notice how it keeps us / in its bounty / while pushing us into the day / dry & proper / pretending we are ready to enter this world / until we find reason to wash again— / I like the moments between past and present / this chrysalis mind / between water & earth / where Time loses power to the baptismal / amniotic / heavy rain / sweat / like the pulse of a dishwasher / the sound of me not on my phone / the skip in my breath as I see a fox by the garden, just waiting to be a poem / & I remember Roland Barthes once said The author enters into his own death, writing begins. / We live but we don't / sometimes we can't. / Like my student's father / who suffered post-COVID psychosis which drove him to Clarks Hill Lake / where he left a note / & tied a car battery to his chest / I imagine him wading out, half wet for a moment / —his hair / I can't stop thinking of it.

Seasons of Anticipation

Matt Gulley

Three moon'd thing
not seasons of weather,

but seasons of anticipation
are always ahead.

For an awaited tv show
or love to arrive, for love to develop
or to end.

How many do you have left?
Is it how you keep time alive?

Each day a color's fraction
within a turning prism.

It's not long now
till it's ages before that many limb'd hand,
Desire

can palm that hot stove,
that burning handle crossed in red

and recoil ugly at the pain
and look to the next season.
Fixed point in the distance,
a welcome sign with fangs.

Trances

L. Ward Abel

We play music behind the lines
of fearful crossings-over,
    those snipers comb
    for people like us

whose herd is culled
through broken ties, wars
an entire generation of charcoal
with names, hard-living
    gone now like
    master and beef.

Our songs now trigger
ten thousand days ago
when we sang atop our lungs
we testified the old ones
    together tethered and
    flowers bloomed

singing without
self-awareness never considered
except as full-voiced trances
    and none of what passes for
    thinking deep.

All those ruins are prelude to
a past come-again
a burned-out block
a silhouette
            but across
            from several gardens

and this ideology in extremis
not good enough to continue
is just enough to be scraps
or midden from washed up
worders, visionaries
            still in hopeful
            remission.

Sister Earth / Leah Dockrill

Flipbooks

Mark Henderson

We're not so much moving
as repeatedly manifesting—

born and dying in rapid succession
under boredom's thumb,

reincarnated as different poses
from the same ol' paper.

We dare hold ourselves to yesterday and tomorrow
beneath the shade of looming pages,

indignant at the backward stares of our pasts.

We come to each other
through the inky pain of the long undrawn,

aching to be what someone else wants
against the flattened fibers—

sped along in dizzy samsara
until we are praying for fire.

Customer

Mark Henderson

I would say I was on break
or it was my first day on the job,
but I don't know what any
of those words mean; I'm just *here*,

and I'd tell you what all of this is surrounding me
if I could tell the difference between sand and water.

Is this a boat or a desk?

A silence explodes, and
I see a dot far off as soon as I think about it.
It's growing, walking, threatening me
with the fact of it—

a Big Bang confronting
with the gravity of its universe,
looking for some sort of explanation.

And I don't know; I just work here.

Senescence

Evan Benedict

Excerpt from The *Ragnarök Cycle*

II. Senescence

Odin spun
from the limbs
of the world-tree,
cast his eyes low, saw the runes
learned their names,
the magic in them
to pass our knowledge,
speak over great distance,

over time.

"Rune" meant "secret,"
sacred knowledge because
words carried starfire and shadow—
light and blight—

breathed magic,
but also wickedness.

And knowledge,
which is both.

"Thus I carve the runes," said he,
to see the future they spelled out.

The word was Ragnarök.
                    His rune. His ruin.

          "Ruin." Latinate and foreign,
but the sound so close,
brushing the back of the neck of rune,
bare syllabic breath, the schwa of "ruin,"
creeping North through the land of Gauls
and quaint Germanic tribes
Great Bear that prowled the sky
to guide the way
so long before the Norsemen came.

"Ruin" predates "rune." How else could it be?
The fall is written in our destiny.
"Fall" is older than "secret."
Older than "rise." Older than "begin."

The Bit That Cannot Be Explained

Jack Stewart

In art there is only one thing that
counts: the bit that cannot be explained.
—Georges Braque

The hedges surrounding the museum
Have grown Cyrillic,
Darkening the last few months.
A man and woman
Stand on the sidewalk
Like seeds for a crowd.
In winter, the stone lions turn Talmudic,
Kippahs of snow on their heads.
Which is holy,
The first touch of brush to canvas
Or the moment it lifts away?
Find the moment between light
And shade and you have
The heartbeat of color,
The voice of God.
You don't need much.
A hedge that is satisfied
With its roots,
A wind that hangs
From branches like fruit and ripens,
Then lets go.

SERENADE / SERGE LECOMTE

Butterfly-cock on Frogs

/ Serge Lecomte

It's a Small World / Serge Lecomte

WHIRLIGIGS

SALLY VENTURA

I once believed my father
practiced the ancient arts,
working with wind, stars, and water.

Instead, he gutted engines,
dug and scraped the ground.
He pulled down the brim of his hat,
lost interest in the dew-sprinkled
webs between rows of corn,
and his hands turned to stone.

So, it was a surprise to find
among clamps, drills, and oil cans,
the wooden whirligigs he had made
before he was buried.

Just a small touch sent their
appendages whirring. The mermaids,
pegged soundly on wooden pedestals,
their bladed arms churning
nothing into nothingness,
and keystone cops, more mustache
than lip, chins parallel with their boots,
slapped with paddle-hands
at the dust they chased:

those silly motions reminding me
that while some part of us stands still,
another part moves the wind ahead,
and I have arrived at the slope of an age
to have stopped fighting
if there is no breeze, to know that
despite the frantic turning, the angel
will never reach the candle
she holds before her, and the blackbird's
steady flight is toward forgiveness.

Woman in the Dressing Glass

Mikal Wix

She comes to feel
That not everything can be glorious,
That no man has mastery over design,
That few moments rise above beginnings
        or finales, that everyone tries
In their own way, even if to open their eyes,
That all the grains of sand or paradise will never,
        ever be enough to arrest the way of ennui,
That on her, some mouths will close
        and some hands open,
That in all the contradictions and behind every
        cold irony, lies one thing
That she'll never reason: why always the pain comes
When all else sleeps, why loss is no borderland
        to race across in search of choice,
And why sometimes the value of a glass to be in
Isn't always open-and-shut, but instead simply
A face to see, a name to call, or a splendor to give,
        as if the stories of all things might one day fall
        back into place, back into a point of origin,
        within her body,
Where even the burning hearts of beasts expelled,
        both infinite and bound, natural or studied,
Can never know the span of time to break the past,
        or the spell to cast
        that opens the very thing needed
                at the instant it's given.

Of Brick

Miriam Borgstrom

to notice her hair was to notice her past / and when she offered herself, the size of her hands differed / if we defined her hair, we would reach zero / the frequency of voices would shatter / once, we attempted sleeping while waking / twice, we attempted new backdrops / and to notice this, has gotten us nowhere / no less than where she began / she forgets the
texture of brick as we become experts on brick
please accept this glove I offer
or accept the glove and call it something else
this is a test on how responsible you are
in a way
in a time of great war between neighboring countries
and neighboring brick
presenting yourself in physical form
presenting a life with room for another life
or simply
replacing our batteries together

NO. 965 FROM SERIES *RANDOM THOUGHTS IN THE WAITING ROOM*

/ K.G. RICCI

WE CAME TO A PLACE THAT WAS GRIEVING AND GATHERED TO LISTEN

IRENE BLAIR HONEYCUTT

CHORUS:

We gather to listen
That the wounded may be healed.
Without stories we lose our way.
What is forgotten will be remembered.
What is buried, unearthed.
Let the litany begin.

LITANY:

I was the minister preaching redemption.
I was the no-see-um in the pulpit.
I was the mantis preying in the offering plate.
I was the genealogy a mother burned in the garden.
I, the black snake, watched from her wash shed.

CHORUS:

There is a time for all
To speak, a time for all
To listen.

LADY LUCK:

I, Lady Luck, for years sat in the
Pews, until one day,
Weary of our liaisons,
I shot the preacher dead.
He dropped like a duck on my lawn.
I was ruled insane, locked away.
So many stories left untold.

MOTHER:

Shall I begin my own litany of doom?
What came after? What went before?

Once I was a leader in that church.
My husband, a deacon—
Finest man I ever knew.
I entertained speakers in our home.
Taught Sunday School. Canned
Tomatoes in the church kitchen.

CHORUS:

We have heard it said
This was not enough.
She craved more.
Each life hungers
For its own experience.

MOTHER:

I ran away from the farm.
Had little education except
In the fields. Married.

Bore children. Sold Avon.
Served appetizers
At Daylight Groceries.
Delivered politicians' pamphlets.
Babysat for doctors' families
Until . . .

Oh, how do I presume?
I ramble in this resume of ruin.
My children—I know they remember
how I tried.
Once a hurricane blew the glass
From the bedroom window.
I sat between them on the bed—
The Bible open in my lap—and prayed.

A few years later at church one night
I wrapped my arms around their shoulders,
Walked between them down the aisle.
Wanted to save them.

Lady Luck's minister (and mine)
Welcomed them into the fold.
He came to our house, too.
As did a friend's husband.
Something cracked inside
My heart. The center
Did not hold.

I became Lady Icarus draped
Over the clothesline
By wagging tongues.

CHORUS:

More than illusion.
More than delusion.
Something other than.
Something deeper than confusion.

MOTHER:

Oh do not ask what happened.
The good Lord knows.
My daughter asked me once,
Sitting next to me on the porch swing,
If I could help her understand.
All I could think to say was:
Loneliness.

People with loose lips blamed my demise,
My fall from the church—my scorn of it—
My agony and crazed state,
On the change of life.
A psychiatrist found my jokes amusing.
Nothing wrong with her, he said,
Returning me to my family waiting
In the lobby. At my own peril
I had become a Master Illusionist.
A Jester even he could not see drowning.

CHORUS:

The Muses say
Women have always tried
To unweave the past,
And have grown old
Trying to imagine a future.

MOTHER:

I will not defile this space.
Will not utter here all I said and did.
What I became   other than this:

I became Lady Arsonist.
Burned the Bible in the backyard.
I became Madam Fury
Fanning the flames.
I became Lady Divinity in the kitchen by day.
Lady Wino in the closet by night.
I became Lady Bagworm
Dragging my home through the streets.
To my children and their father
I became the ghost that never died.

DAUGHTER:

Sometimes she comes as chimes on the   wind
Becomes choruses of frogs   in   swamp   lands
Sometimes she reaches   for   blushing   lilies
Sometimes floats   on   buoyant   leaves
She becomes spoonbills stepping into cool   waters
Becomes ghost beads   rattling   inside Peruvian shakers
Becomes a mouse   poised   in an   alley
Becomes trees   whispering   secrets
To   nameless   stones.

LITANY:

We, the humming birds she fed, tallied her visits.
We, the bees, pollinating flowers, recognized her face.
We, the willows, wept with her when she stretched out on our roots.

MOTHER:

My daughter,

When you thought you were lost
I guided you.
When you thought you were alone
I brought you home.
I picked up the prayers
You dropped on the rug.
I became the talking stick
You held in your hand.
Became the drum
You could not stop beating.
Wherever you go I am there.
You carry me—a waxing moon
at your back.

Speculum Lacum / Robert Palmer

Lessons

Chris Fleming

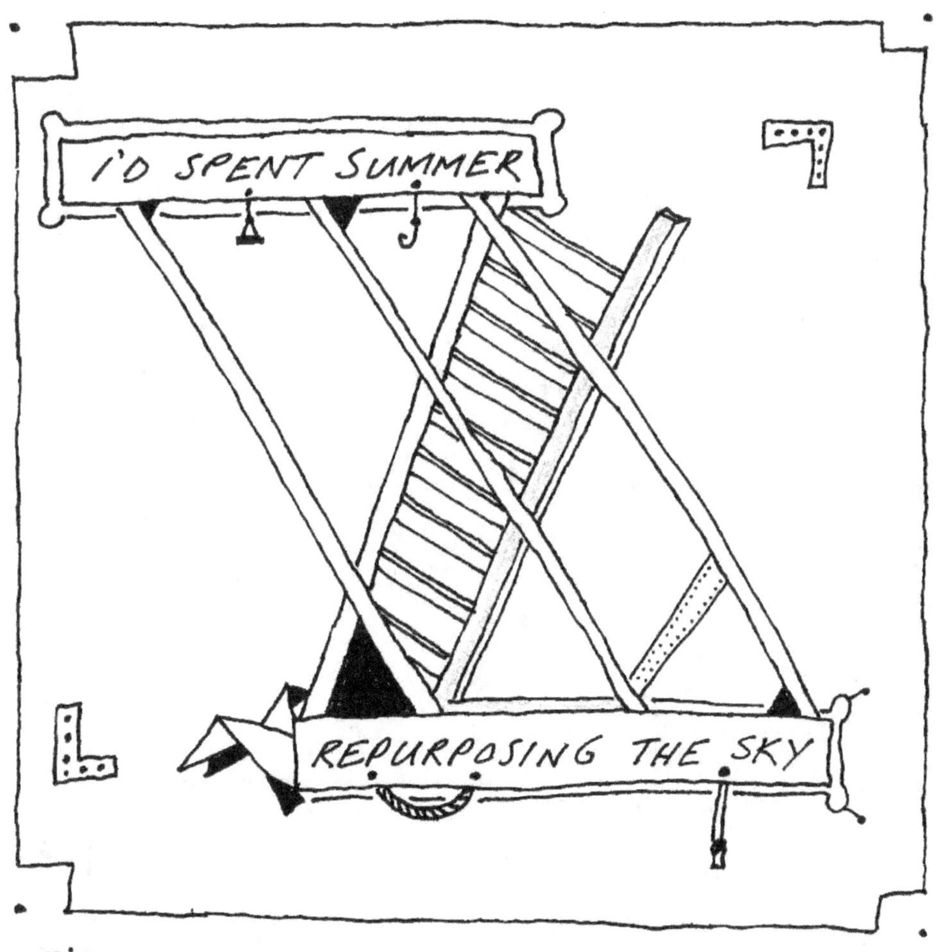
I'D SPENT SUMMER
REPURPOSING THE SKY

RETROFITTING CLOUDS WITH HOOKS,
HANDLES, AND DROP-DOWN ROPES

HAVING COMPLETED THIS TO MY SATISFACTION,
TO MOVED ON TO PARKLANDS, FORESTS,
SURROUNDING RESERVES - GIFTING TREES
LITTLE ORIGAMI
BIRDS, LADDERS,
AND LIGHTS.

THEY WERE LONG DAYS
AND I LABOURED ALONE

THEN SOMETHING SHIFTED UNDER THE SKIN, SOME DARK CHEMICAL UNCOUPLING, TITRATION OF WILL. I CLIMBED DOWN, PACKED MY THINGS, AND RETURNED.

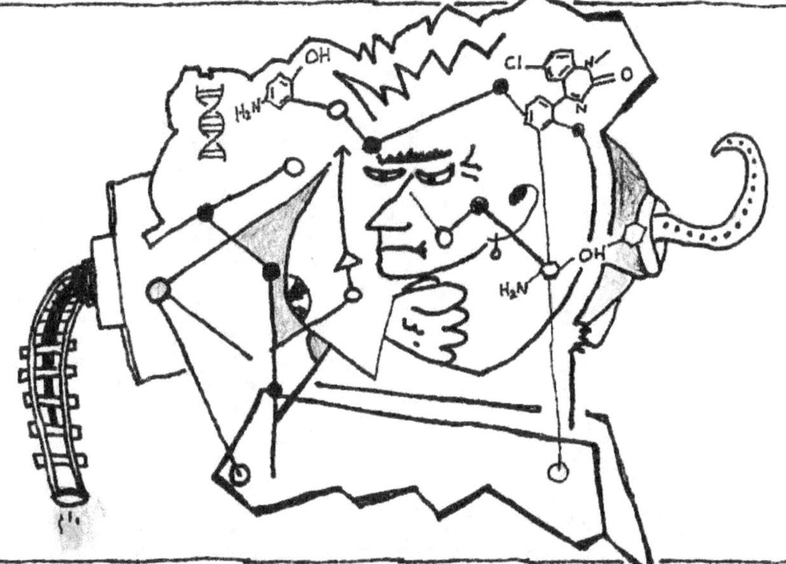

MY HANDS WERE THICK AND COARSE, THE CORNERS OF MY EYES CREASED, MY FACE BROWN. I LOOKED IN THE MIRROR. I WAS STRANGE TO MYSELF.

THEN YOU CAME TO TOWN AND DIDN'T SEE - OR TOOK NO NOTICE. OR MAYBE YOU SAW BUT SAID NOTHING.
ALL FINE, OF COURSE. I'D NEVER UPSET MYSELF ABOUT THIS.
NONE OF IT WAS FOR YOU, ANYWAY.

THEN YOU LEFT AND I RETURNED
TO SURVEY MY WORK AND PHOTOGRAPHED
IT ALL; MAYBE, I THOUGHT, IN AID
OF OFFERING A SET OF LESSONS-
ABOUT AN HONEST DAY'S WORK, SAY,
OR ABOUT GOALS AND VISION AND
WHAT IS POSSIBLE. OF A FULL HUMAN
LIFE.

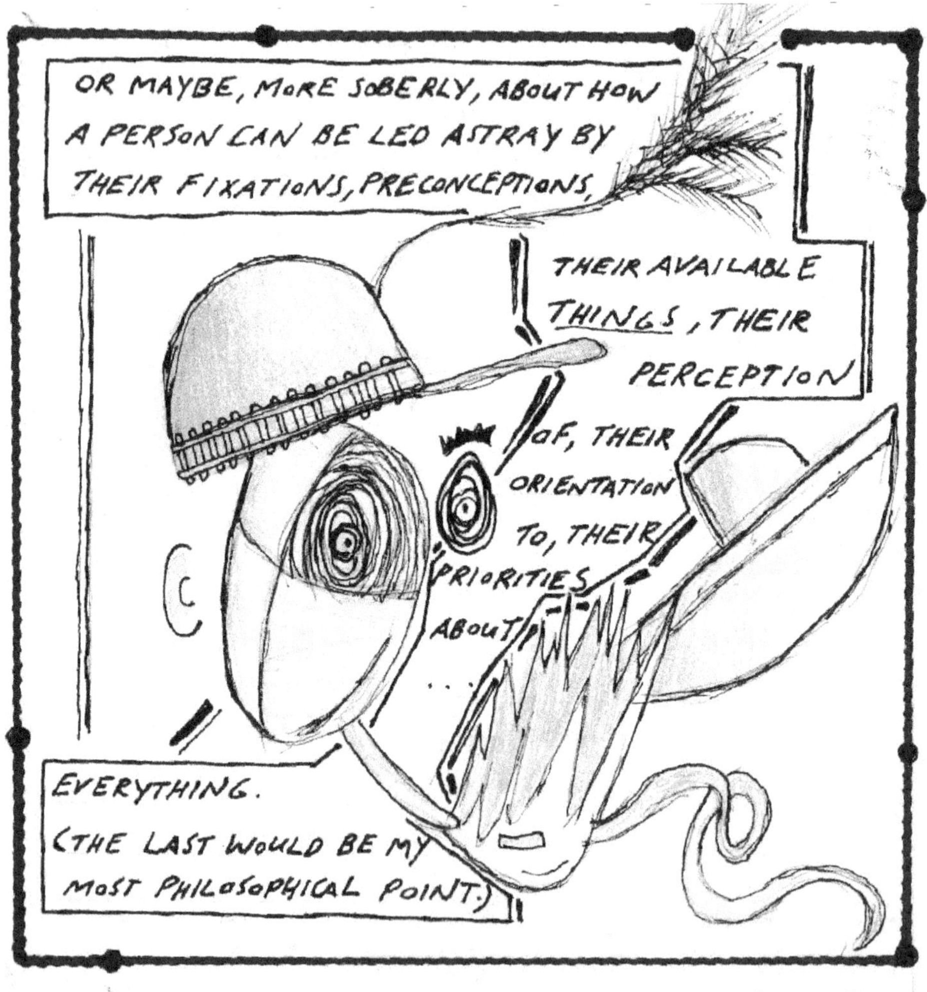
OR MAYBE, MORE SOBERLY, ABOUT HOW A PERSON CAN BE LED ASTRAY BY THEIR FIXATIONS, PRECONCEPTIONS,
THEIR AVAILABLE THINGS, THEIR PERCEPTION
OF, THEIR ORIENTATION TO, THEIR PRIORITIES ABOUT
...
EVERYTHING.
(THE LAST WOULD BE MY MOST PHILOSOPHICAL POINT.)

YOU RETURNED ONE LAST TIME IN JANUARY

I LIT AN OIL BURNER, ARRANGED LAMPS WITH THEATRICAL PRECISION, AND TRIED TO HOLD YOUR GAZE OVER TEA. WE SMILED OFTEN AND YOU LAUGHED TWICE. IT WAS NORMAL, ADULT, CIVIL, NICE-NICE ENOUGH. AND YOU CERTAINLY DIDN'T HAVE TO REACT: OUTLINE OF MY NEW TAKE, THE LESSON, ROUNDED 2, EVIDENCE, PEDAGOGICAL APPROACH, USE OF COLOUR.

IT WASN'T YOU I WANTED TO TEACH,
AFTER ALL...

I DONT KNOW WHY I MENTION IT.

(EVEN SO.)

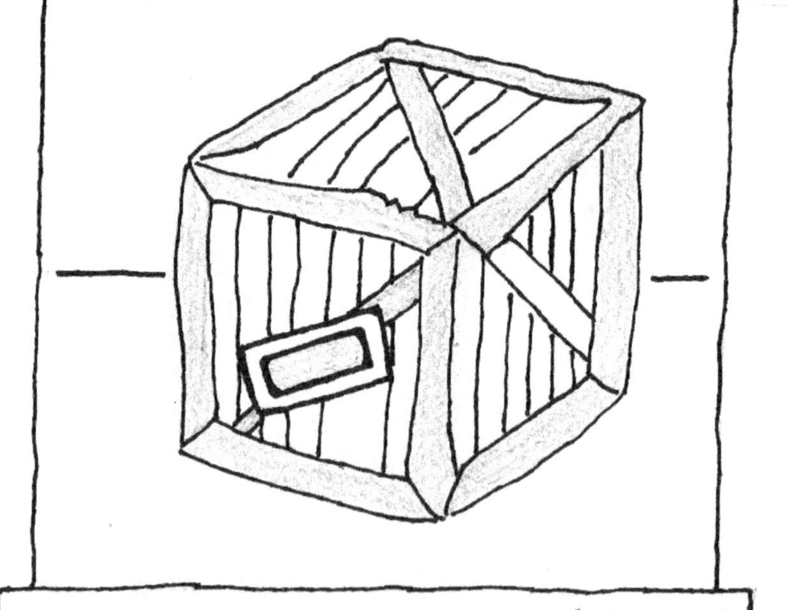
I'VE DECIDED I WILL TEAR IT ALL DOWN ONE YEAR FROM NOW. I WILL PACK IT AND STORE IT IN THE FLAT WHERE WE USED TO LIVE, AND PEOPLE CAN COME AND LOOK.
THERE WILL BE NO ADMISSION CHARGE.

x
AND THEN I'LL START AGAIN.

UNTITLED, FROM THE *FACING IT TOGETHER* SERIES / JACK BORDNICK

Our Obit

Aarron Sholar

Quarterly Editor's Prize

(b.1999)

I would sit on the queen-sized bed in the guest room, dressed in a pair of pajama pants and a long t-shirt. The bed faced a simple mirror and a dark wooden bookshelf, which held an endless number of books to pick from each night. One day, mom brought me a book that had a magenta sleeve, maybe with some yellow as well, with a picture of a young girl on the front. Mom sat beside me and began to explain what the doctor had said about me being an early bloomer. She explained the process of puberty, what would happen, and that it's normal. She asked me if I had questions before bed, and she happily disproved the utterly confused question of *does a hole show up in my side and just bleed? Will it close up after?*

In the seventh or eighth grade, I asked my mom how to shave my legs, like all the other middle school girls had begun to do. I imagine her face lit up as she explained the process to me: how you should lather your legs up with soap, go against the way the hair falls to be sure you get it all, *but be careful* she warned me, *it'll get addicting—you'll want to get every last hair.* I probably smiled back at her, nodding, trusting her words of experience. I still hear her words every time I shave my face.

Mom also read non-puberty books to me on that bed. When I was even younger, before I could read reliably, she showed me her favorite book series, *The Chronicles of Narnia*. They felt and looked old, they even *smelled* old, but I nestled beside her on that bed as she'd read the chapter for the night. She never read in silly voices for different characters, as some parents might; instead, she just used her own voice. I'd watch her flip every browning page, each one releasing more of the book's relaxing, albeit ancient, odor. Some nights I never wanted her to stop reading—this was our connection, books. I was the only sibling out of the three of us who actually liked them.

Mom would stand in the kitchen every Thursday night as she washed dishes and cleaned up post dinner. She had her drying towel in one hand, a plate in the other, being dried, and a green and yellow spelling book on the granite countertop in front of her. She goes down the list of vocab words for that week, protruding them at me with her voice: *definition, exempt, discipline*! I'd write all ten on my loose-leaf paper for her to check afterwards. If I got any wrong, she'd have me verbally spell out every word on the list back to her instead of writing them. If I got them all right during our practice, I could go play video games.

Mom drove my sister and I to McDonald's every month or so for a treat. We'd actually go into the building and not just through the drive thru, as she knew this was more exciting to us. I got the same meal every time, six-piece chicken nuggets with a boy toy. I'd peel the semi-hard skin away, eating it before consuming the pale meat, all while playing with the *Narnia* Happy Meal toy I'd gotten this time. This series of toys had ended before I was able to collect all of them, so my mom dug through eBay to purchase the rest of them. After a few weeks, I could reenact the rising of Aslan properly, over and over.

Mom eventually got me my own, newer *Narnia* book set; this set came in a sleek box with shiny, gold lettering and a picture of the Dawn Treader on each side. The books were sleek too, the covers featuring reimagined pictures of series events, such as battles or major characters. This time, I read through them in my own voice. While I loved the stories, I was more so fascinated by them because mom loved them. I see now that I wanted to be closer to her—to not only see *why* she loved these books for myself, but to see a part of *her* in them.

(d. 2015)

In my junior year of high school, I stopped shaving my legs. Come the Spring, my cargo shorts displayed my leg hair to the whole school. My mom's once wide smile from those years ago was gone as she drove off to my sister and I's weekly music lessons without me. It was the hair. If I wouldn't wear pants, I wouldn't leave the house, is what I understood it as. From the front window, I watched as my mom sped away in the minivan. My violin sat beside me as I wondered what she told my violin teacher. Maybe I'd come down with a cold, maybe I'd injured myself somehow. I decided that I *was* not to be seen.

I sat on the loveseat, a pillow on each end; my mom sat in front and to the right of me, my gender therapist in front and to the left. My mom held a folded-up sheet of loose-leaf paper, the one I'd spent a week scribbling all over; this sheet of paper revealed to her that I was a boy. She had a smile on her face as I locked eyes with her, but her words said the opposite: *I'm not going to call you that.* My hands, which I had forced under my thighs, began to sweat, my skin sticking together. Although she knew why I had stopped shaving, I was still not allowed in public with those legs. They were still the most disrespectful thing she had ever encountered.

Maybe a year later, my therapist suggested I offer a book to my mom, to help her understand what I was going through; that book was *Some Assembly Required*, the one I had read just after realizing that being transgender was possible and a legit medical thing with a diagnosis and everything. That book gave me hope for a future, and I wanted it to do the same for her. I left it on her desk with a note on top of it. Not a day later, it was on her bookshelf, unread—the note removed.

Still, I decided that I wanted to ask my mom to come with me to my hormone therapy consult with me. I walked into the

kitchen, the struggling starting up again. Mom tended to do this thing where if she didn't seem to want to come to terms with something, she'd just ignore it, hoping it would eventually go away. My arms rested on the green granite where that vocab book once sat: *Mom, can you come to my consult with me next week?* She stopped doing the dishes, the clang of plates and silverware sudden under the water of the sink. She didn't even turn to look at me: *No, it's just sad.* Her voice seemed to falter some, distressed. There's silence. And then: *This is important to me, please?* She begins washing again. *No, it's not important, it's just sad.*
I left.

A week later, my mom sat in the examination room with the doctor and I as we discussed hormone replacement therapy, going over all the ins and outs. The room was sterile in every way —the smell of alcohol wipes stung our noses; the air we breathed was stale; our voices seemed to echo within the room; the paper sheet I sat on felt extra paper-y, more intense. My mom sat in the corner, her arms crossed against her chest and her eyes never meeting the doctor's. But, she asks—*Does she have to do this for the rest of her life? How does it affect fertility?* She may have been unhappy, sad, as she'd said in the kitchen, but she was here, asking questions. She was present, at the least. And I appreciated that.

The day I was to have my double mastectomy, my mom and I both zombied out of bed at 4 a.m., got dressed, and wandered into the car. I remember laying in that moving hospital bed, the soft fabric of my gown brushing against my body; it reminded me of why I was there—these breasts didn't belong, they caused too much pain. My mom came into the "room," really just an open space divided up by swinging curtains. She sat beside me, but I can't remember if she held my hand or not. I had to ask her for a hug before I was wheeled away. She gave me one, telling me *I'll see you soon, I'm going to get some coffee.* I told her that was a good idea; a nurse recommended some nearby coffee places.

On the car ride home, she told me that that hospital, George Washington in DC, was the one she was also born in, all those years ago. Isn't that funny? My mom was born in the same place a part of me died.

After my surgery, my mom was not necessarily happy to help with recovery, but she was *there* to help. She collected items off kitchen shelves for me that I couldn't reach, she stood beside me in every bathroom in the house, emptying my drains into a red solo cup (*yum*) before dumping the bodily sludge into the toilet before flushing. She made sure I was taken care of, but—

There were rules for my new body around the house: out of the shower, I still had to wear my towel wrapped around where my breasts would be; I wasn't allowed to be shirtless in front of anyone else in the house. I felt like I couldn't bring it up in any way. It was over, done with, so I had to ignore that it ever happened too, just like mom did. Regardless of her help, I was still she, I was still [redacted]. But this went on for years, so I'd get used it; so much so that I'd ignore my own feelings of fake love. of rejection.

(b. d. 2021)

Finally, I sent my mom a letter. The letter detailed my feelings from the last couple of years: I appreciated her newfound support; I was originally OK with my original name being used around the house; I was fine with being a *she* at home— but it wasn't OK anymore. Those words held memories, memories like being held home from school due to my unshaven legs, like my mom telling me how sad it is what I'm doing. I wanted to be that little girl in bed with my mom, reading peacefully, but a boy —I wanted that relationship back.

Mom called me on my way to work: *so I got your letter —*
and we talked about it. I could hear her smile come back as she spoke:

Why didn't you just tell me that you were so upset? I didn't think you cared.

Do you want me to call you Aarron?
Yes, dear God, please.

. . .

I love you, Aarron.

I was back in that bed with her. She was reading *Voyage of the Dawn Treader*, the part where one of the men at the table exclaimed "mustard please!" for some reason I don't remember, but that was my favorite part of the book (I was very upset it was not in the movie). I asked her to read it again, so she started the page over. I'd read this scene to myself a couple of years later. Maybe I should dig that collection out and read it through again.

(b. 2021 —)

She hasn't messed up my name since.

COVID COLOR SET 2H / CYNTHIA YATCHMAN

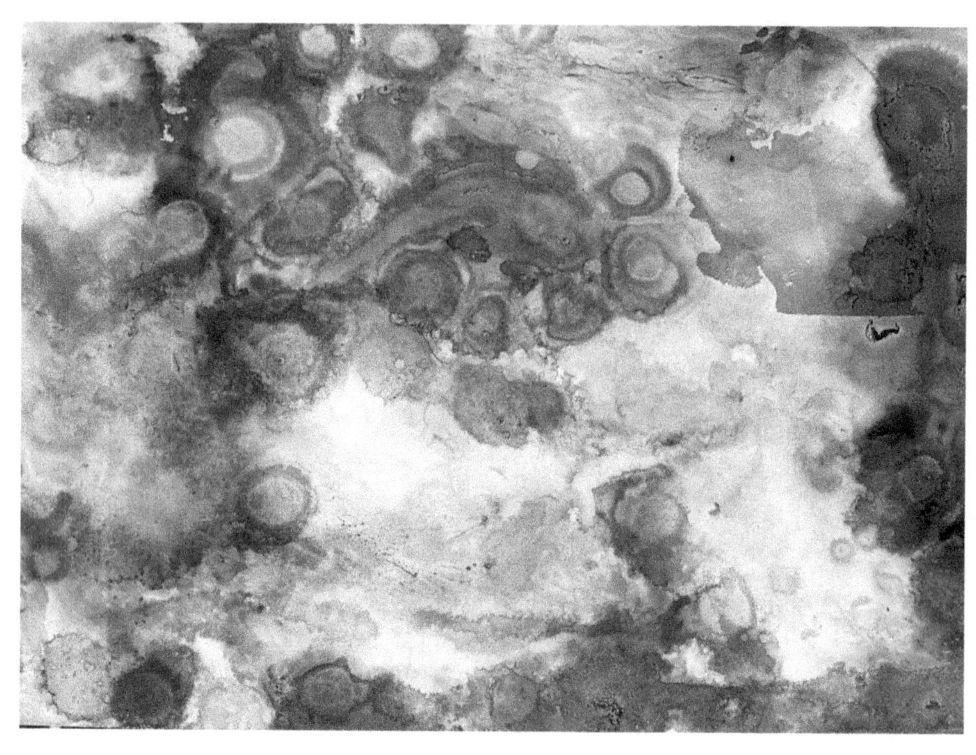

COVID COLOR SET 2L / CYNTHIA YATCHMAN

Something In the Water

Federica Santini

It just rained and the ground smells of new births and ashes. The bottle is half buried and cracked. Held in its uneven mouth, barely visible: two opaque beads *(my eyes?)*, leaves not quite burned by the season *(the polish has splintered on my fingertips)*, rain-darkened weeds *(my hair is matted, unruly)*, a single green blade chanting softly in tune with my voice, which I hear but cannot recognize. Soil all around, a broken doll's hand *(my own broken hand? Another's?)*. Everything that hurts is in the bottle.

Can water hurt? Small white faces peer from the branches, staring at me. The day the pill bank at the station shut down, everyone screaming and rushing out, he said he'd go for a vasectomy. Next morning, the news came that they made that illegal along with all body alterations. I took off my earrings, he slid off his tongue piercing. I started covering my tattoo with long-sleeved tops—it's best to display modesty in any case, though there has been no ban. No matter now, I no longer go out. We stopped sex for a while, thought of other ways for intimacy, our limbs intertwined in our dreams.

Then the supplements arrived in the mail for non-mothers, to help us conceive. You have to take two every night with dinner. Just vitamins, B12, nothing harmful. It's what every woman should take. Every new cycle, I see another small face lurking, white and jeering. They say it's my conscience, the unconceived babies calling for me. They say I'm murdering them every month. He said it's all in my head. But I think there must be something in the water. The water comes free with the supplements, a special treat for us non-mothers. I threw out the first pills, and got fined. Then the fines got higher, the check-ins tighter. Weekly blood sampling, bounty hunters out to seek those who do not comply, those who do not conceive. I complied. The small white faces began popping up at the edge of my vision. He said it's all in my head. I say there's something in the water.

I look at that first bottle, half-hidden in the garden, the two pills like glassy eyes just inside it. Small faces circle around like eerie glowworms, yet it's full day. Everything that hurts is in the bottle, hard to dislodge or unearth. Hidden deep in the bottle there's me, waiting, whole and unseen.

YOU DO NOT STOP AT YOUR SKIN

SUNNY PAYSON

It is the missing checkbook register. Proof, for the first time, that Diana had been taken, examined, done things to, and returned promptly at the exact moment she'd been extracted. At 12:23 p.m., she notices the checkbook register is missing. She had just recorded check #1034, remitted for pest services rendered. She had not risen from the chair. She had barely moved. It is not on her desk, nor at her feet. She searches around her workstation, flipping through books and shaking out legal pads that lay in orderly stacks, and the register is nowhere to be found. Her face burns with a new kind of pride. She is entangled, being called for this experience, finding, after all this time, that she is right, that she is truly a special being, a true starseed, meant for something on this earth.

How it was somehow overlooked, dropped from her hand, gently, to the floor. Perhaps hidden in darkness under the examination table, its worn pages, the bent staples that barely held it together, the numbers she'd scrawled diligently, because Jason would not be happy if he knew she hadn't kept up. Diana never forgot how he looked at her after seeing the scribbled withdrawals paired with unmarked balance columns.

What, she'd said, I can always check at the ATM.

He had been gentle, though, even though he was under a great deal of stress launching his new business. He'd grab her by the waist as she walked by his transitional office space, part of the living room near the kitchen, and spin her around on his lap, while she gripped the back rest, the room spiraling.

The shed he'd built for his office is almost finished. The splotches of joint compound sanded smooth and the unprimed drywall waiting for paint, solidly upright, not crooked like the walls of the small farmhouse they share with a semi-hostile housemate. She is like a teenager most of the time, drifting by in pajamas looking at her phone, on the way in or out of her room.

When they'd converted part of the living room for Jason's workspace, she'd dragged the love seat into her room, claiming that the living room wasn't hers to hang out in anymore, and unless they wanted less rent, they would agree to it. Which was fine, it ended up working out, most of the time, with Jason in front of his computer, lines of code and text that Diana couldn't, nor did she want to try and decipher. She preferred their bedroom anyway, facing south, where the slant of orange light in the afternoon turns oblique, strikes a distinct diagonal line from the window to her bed, where her polished crystals are arranged on the nightstand and her embroidered pillows soften the wooden headboard and her thinking mind. And the small, rounded skylight, her keyhole to the clouds.

Even through the smoky and pale sky, a wishful kind of a blue, she senses the density of what is situated beyond it, that great black ocean, dotted with infinite pinholes, and beyond that, well, she is investigating those realms without her conscious awareness. Diana had been past what is known to man, and her body had opened to it, like a quickening.

Diana M. from Santa Rosa purchased a Community Learn/ Grow Your Group Workshop.
Serena K. from East LA purchased a personal tarot reading.
Aline P. from Calabasas purchased a hand crafted Shungite Pyramid.

Diana slips the credit card back into her wallet, pleased to have found the website. Pleased that the cost isn't too high. She is not alone, wanting to create a community in her own town, in which she knows few people.

This workshop is a good start. A fresh start. Anything is possible in a constructed world, she whispers. Her life inside the farmhouse is hermetic, and good things happen when she leaves it, when she is paying close enough attention.

A rainbow stretches across the highway, the arc getting lost in the haze, and then suddenly, brilliant, hovering over the grocery store. Diana pulls into the parking lot, imagining the automatic doors shattering, gold coins spilling out across the pavement, rushing through the streets with ringing change.

She parks the car and goes in. Rows of garden shovels, neatly spooning, hung on rubberized steel rods next to the perennials sale. How many shovelfuls of gold could she put in the trunk? Separating a mini shopping cart from the row, she has to pull hard and two others come with it. Before pushing them back, she sees a twenty, folded tightly in quarters, in the bottom of the cart. She slips it into the outer pocket of her jeans, feels the thickness between her fingers. Could be sixty dollars. Good as gold. As the doors slide shut behind her, and the long aisle of refrigerated perishables stretches out in front of her, she catches a chill, and her body slows. Trapped in air like water. The cold lights overhead bring out the yellow undertones of her skin. She is looking at her hands, curled around the greasy handle of the cart, when she realizes she is unable to move at all.

And she remembers. She has been here before. Not déja vu, but this trajectory she's already completed: this time of day, this same light outside, this oily shopping cart. She examined the backs of her hands exactly like this the last time. Her body is sending messages and she can't understand what they mean. Why she is stuck in place? Why are the lights suddenly not like lights but like paint, pouring from above, and the floor is suddenly mostly like liquid. It's a good thing, she thinks, that I have hold on this cart. But it's like someone is saying it to her, inhabiting her, while she is still present.

Can I help you? A woman in a royal blue smock comes close to her. Diana moves just her eyes to see the face, reads a name tag on her shoulder. Lisa. Weird place for a name tag.

Can I help you? Are you alright?

Lisa's breath smells like she doesn't drink enough water. She waves her hand in front of Diana's eyes. Diana blinks. She hears her own voice, not her real voice, squeeze up out of herself, as if her body is trying to keep it from escaping.

I am fine.

Her voice sounds garbled, though clear enough, but she stays stuck in place, leaning on the cart for support, and so, does not convince Lisa. Diana wonders if she looks pale. When was the last time she ate? Lisa takes out a small, ergonomic walkie talkie, and calls for someone in customer service, which Diana hears in the air in front of her, and after a delay, bouncing across the ceiling and the white sprayed I beams above.

Families slump by in groups, the kids belted into jumbo size carts, kicking at their parents, grabbing the styrofoam packages of bacon, throwing them at the floor. An older sibling smacks the side of their head and picks up the meat, tosses it back in the cart.

Sleepwalkers. The bloated focus in the mother's eyes sharpens as she drifts past Diana, briefly glancing at Lisa, and moving on. The teenager lags behind, neck bent to see her phone. Her mouth is parted as she scrutinizes an image and makes it larger with two fingers. Diana can see the screen as she passes. Coral pink bikini top. Glacially brilliant teeth. Plush pink lips, absent of detail, gleaming.

It all repeats itself like a broken piece of code, in this shambolic simulation. That's what Jason calls it, and Diana believes him. She's seen black cats double and split, slink off in opposite directions in kaleidoscopic symmetry. She expects she'll see another family turn the corner, the bacon will fall, the slap, the mother, the teenager, the phone, the bikini, the teeth.

Lisa is joined by another smock wearing employee, a grey-haired woman holding a price tag gun. Her name tag is right over her chest. Eliza.

Did you page?

You're not customer service, where is Barbara?

I am Barbara today.

Your name tag says Eliza, Diana says quietly.

Lisa may have heard but she is involved with telling Eliza what has happened. She is referring to Diana as the customer. Diana stops listening and watches as another family passes, this time from another direction, as they walk away from her. A jug of milk tumbles out of the cart. The dad smacks the kid on the side of the head. The mother leans over and picks it up, carefully placing the dented gallon under the cart, on its side. A teenager follows.

Diana experiments with small, light steps, and the cart inches in retreat. It's not like she can't move, but a feeling that she shouldn't. That she has been changed in ways she doesn't yet understand, like after a long yoga class, lying in savasana, absorbing the benefits. She is certain that Lisa would not understand and she won't bother to try and explain. Lisa and Eliza are still trying to figure out the proper protocol. Lisa hunches over her walkie talkie, tries to hide the fact that she is paging a supervisor, which Diana can clearly hear echoing back to them.

Aisle Three, Supervisor, customer concern, please.

Diana continues until she is a good fifteen feet away, and quickly swivels into aisle four, Spices/Pasta/Tomato Sauce/ International Food. She doesn't remember what she was supposed to buy. Digging in her pockets, only after she's reached the meat counter, does she find a list. The handwriting looks different from her own. More like her mother's careful letters.

Yes ma'am, what can I get you today?

Diana smiles at the man, snapping back into herself. His voice has a quality she recognizes, but not from where.

I'll take the farmed salmon please, enough for two people. She straightens her back, unties her fleece jacket from around her waist and puts it on.

Yeah, I wear extra pairs of socks working back here. All this ice. And the cooler. He gestures behind him, towards a scuffed up white wall. The metal door to the cooler hangs open. Several dents mar its dimpled surface, as if someone had hammered at it from the inside. Another man in a white coat with his back to them is wrestling with something unwieldy, lumpen. His body resembles a small boulder, rolling around an uneven floor.

Diana tunes her attention, watches the man at the counter laying out the filet across the white plastic cutting board, gently angling the edge of the knife to the fatty orange slab.

How much? Here?

Yes, she says, as she glances at his hands.

He sinks the blade into the fish while letting his eyes rest on Diana.

It is darker outside than when she arrived. The air is acrid still, with the distant fires, casting a dim blue veil over the rows of cars. To the far left of the sliding doors, by the loading dock, two seated figures smoke cigarettes. They do not speak. They are observing her. The long strips of vinyl swish in and out.

She slams the trunk shut. The lights above flicker on. A low buzzing noise finds its chorus and the entire lot swarms with expanding pools of light. She is thinking of the meat counter guy and wonders if she knows him, already.

Jason is in bed reading on his phone when she gets home. One light on the nightstand points at the doorway, so she can't see his face.

What's for dinner babe?

Fish

Which kind?

Armchair.

Alright.

After dinner, as she's wiping dry the last plates, Diana tries to crystallize her afternoon, as it actually happened. She can't remember what exactly had occurred before she was frozen in place. It seems absurd that she was being treated like an old woman with dementia, or whatever deemed it necessary for those pushy women to immediately rush up to her, to try and keep her moving along. She recalls the events in order, rainbow, money, sliding doors, and then blank. She reaches into her jeans pocket and pulls out the bills. She was right; it was sixty dollars. She smiles widely and slides the money back in her pocket.

Jason rounds the corner into the kitchen, a thick joint over his lip, clicks on the burner and leaning low to one side, lights it in a few puffs.

What are you smiling about?

Nothing, just happy, Diana says.

He walks over to her, wraps his arms around her, her face at his chest. While keeping one arm around her shoulders, he takes a thick drag, touches her lips with his own. When she opens her mouth he exhales, and while she breathes in she forgets whatever she was trying to do, to remember. It was useless anyway.

Let's get out of the kitchen, babe. A plume of skunky smoke follows him back into the living room.

Diana pours two glasses of water, can hear Jason's voice but not his words. She flicks off the bright lights.

. . . would've done it differently, he says from the couch, inhaling the smoke with a low hissing sound, then holding it in as he keeps talking.

A seamless design structure isn't necessarily the best design, it's basically irrelevant.

He lets out the cloud of smoke in a controlled release.

Weighs down the whole system and that's what causes the glitches, the big ones, that shouldn't exist in such great numbers. The ones even the sleepwalkers notice. What you've absolutely got to do, is to get the details perfect and let the seams be like air, like little blank thought bubbles. Let people fill them in, let people see that cat cross their path, but not again the same day. What a sham.

He takes another lengthy drag off the joint, runs his other hand through his hair, feeling the base of his neck, and closing his eyes briefly, exhales, and time stretches the room away from him.

Diana sits quietly, waiting. She wants the conversation to go into the subject of original design and theoretical control keepers. Right now, she really wants to tell him about the checkbook register, about the edgeless experience of traveling without knowing, and to ask him, what do you think, where do you think I was?

He looks over at his computer, and back at Diana.

Come here, babe, and he pats the couch next to him. She fits herself close into the side of his body, which he angles towards her, as he passes her the joint. There isn't much left, she takes a quick puff, barely able to pinch the sticky crinkle of paper at the end, trying not to burn her lips. The room sinks down while she exhales. The ceiling disappears. She leans her head back against the couch.

In the bathroom, she flips on the light and starts to floss her teeth without looking in the mirror. She hasn't seen her own face all day. The shower curtain is closed. She edges away from it. Closing her eyes, and rips it aside. A spider runs across the smooth white vinyl, tries to climb the wall, slides down again. It could be that the floor is sinking and the walls are lengthening.

The light is out in the bedroom. Jason reaches for her, his body animal with early sleep, and he pulls her to him. His hand brushes over her stomach, as he slips his palm under her t-shirt, over her breasts. His fingers are warm and smooth. They weren't always. When he'd done construction, she could barely have him touch her. But he'd get home early, and they would shower together, fucking while standing up in the stall, the skin on his hands softening under the hot water. She missed that. There was no roommate then, either.

Jason pulls at her underwear, his fingers already seeking.

No, not yet she says, turning her back, and his hand retreats from between her legs, goes back to her breasts. His lips against her ear, how about now, he whispers, now, he repeats. Her skin is getting warm and she pulls her t-shirt over her head. His body pools into hers, sleek against her back. His hand smooths over her hip, trails down. His fingers stroking her on the outside, and she giggles a little. Diana feels like an animal, something cute, something adorable, and she is also getting wet. She pushes herself into him and he slides his fingers into her, and it feels good in a way she hasn't had it in a while. Maybe because the roommate isn't there, maybe because Jason waited longer for her, she doesn't know and is trying to turn off her brain when she feels something she would later describe as familiar,

A dark smudge of something like a man drifts in the hall, not quite there, not quite man, but a trail of a man, an idea of a man's body. She sees him just in the corner of her eye, and of course, as always when she sees what is and isn't there, he disappears. What doesn't make sense is that she is not startled, nor afraid, and while not unexpected, her body remembers. Not everything, but like a frame from a movie, filmed while she wasn't watching.

Where'd you go, babe?

Diana wonders. They start up again.

Jason is fucking her from behind, and she is trying, as always, to slow him down, to get into his rhythm, and the man-not man reappears. This time, directly beneath her as a darkish swarm and his hands-not hands are close, his fingers forming a buzzing arc just above Jason's cock; a dome or a hive of warmth and everything good, this sensation of movement and buzzing and mostly humming, like a body hums and rises, ringing at a frequency reserved for dreams and how a body feels in dreams, without specific sensorial detail, without the recording of smell or the contact of skin.

She shifts her weight from her hands to her forearms, turns her tongue in slow circles as if to discover a new shape. A brief and bitter taste registers in her mouth, like a spark, and then fades as she starts to come. There seems to be no end to her, no resistance, only a blazing pulse she cannot bear and doesn't want to stop.

After Jason pulls out and slumps into the space next to Diana, it is as if he's been dropped out of the sky. She remains stone still, lying on her stomach and holding her breath, trying not to disturb the warmth under her belly, hoping to keep something of the man-not man with her. She is being tricked into something, a vague dart at the back of her mind whistles, slicing through the vapor and breath of the chatter in her brain.

Any heart palpitations or blurred vision?

No.

Any headaches or memory loss?

No.

Anything you might be worried about at this time, or mental health concerns?

The nurse taps out Diana's answers. It seems to her the amount of letters clicking away exceeds the amount of words she uses. The monitor is positioned away from her. An uncovered bank of fluorescents provides scant light and several of the milky grey tubes seem to contain fluttering insects. Diana presses her hands together, thumbs interlocked, like she does at the dentist. She kneads her palm on the underside with one thumb, as hard as she can stand it. The steady pressure keeps her calm. She tries it during the blood pressure screening. No luck, 130 over 82.

Married, single, partner?

Yes, I live with my boyfriend.

She is a little proud when she says this, imagining Jason at home, building his company, bit by bit. He is so focused, that when she comes home, he hasn't even gotten up to drink water, his lips dry when she first kisses him, his phone lit up with messages and the snaking lines of code streaming down the front of his computer, like the stones of a building, rising, rising.

Contraception?

The nurse has stopped typing and is looking directly at Diana for the first time, speaking to her as if to a child after having repeated herself. Opaque turquoise eyeshadow shimmers against her dark skin.

What?

What form of birth control do you use?

The air in the room tightens around Diana, as it always does right before she lies. The walls bend convex behind the examination table, its stirrups like arms, reaching.

I'm on the pill.

OK, and the dosage?

Oh, I forget, I've been taking it so long.

The nurse stops typing again and looks at Diana, her hands still poised at the keyboard, her nails lacquered and sharp. They are briefly locked together, two lambs. The nurse doesn't hide her reaction, rolls her eyes, and slides the keyboard table back under the screen, which blinks out and is replaced by a lazily bouncing logo.

The doctor will be with you shortly, the nurse says into the air. She closes the door gently behind her. A slow click. Diana's clothes sway lightly on the plastic hangers on the back of the door.

Diana begins to cry, and is unsure why she is here in the first place. The annual. It's simply what we do, she had remembered. She looks down into her lap, her fingers all twisted together, her legs pressing into each other. Her crossed feet look unlike her own, resting against the speckled linoleum squares. Her body wants out.

She stands up, slips on her sandals, throws her jacket over her head, over the paper gown, and runs out the of the exam room, hugging her keys and clothes and wallet and phone to her chest. A different nurse pauses in the hallway, in slow and subtle movement, turns her body to see Diana. Her look is unsurprised. The heavy bar of the exit door clunks down and the pitch of alarm sounds waver on, then cut out as the door slams shut.

There is an empty field, an incongruous stretch of prairie near the freeway, that Diana has passed on her way in or out of the city more times than she can remember. And each time she passes it, she promises she will pull over the next time, and walk right into the center of it. There is a concentration of spectacular energy, multiplied by the thousands of wheat-colored stalks, either created in their susurration when the wind picks up, or perhaps the oddity of the non-native grasses themselves, originating from a thousand miles away, spread like a silk rug, woven in secret. That its power comes from its indifference, this square plot of land, seemingly owned by no one, unmarked or fenced in any way. An invitation, a wayshower stamped into the earth, for those who are looking, those who can see.

It is night now, and Diana cautiously drives onto the shoulder, into the border of the grasses, her headlights reaching no further than the first thick rows. Cars shave close as they zip by, hurry home. She wriggles across the interior of the car, exits from the passenger side.

A silent red light, blinking across the western edge of the night sky, drops off from Diana's field of vision, as she tries to expand the peripheral edge of what she can see. The limits are too close, she thinks, the field too narrow to capture signals, or to send them with her positive mind stream. She breathes in deeply to clear her body of any webby darkness, any doubts that might stain her consciousness. They do not reach out to human bodies in discord.

A semi truck downshifts off the curve in the highway. She can't see it, but the bridge is only a few hundred yards away. It is late and the traffic has subsided. She doesn't check her phone, the brightness of the screen will ruin her eyes for the night. She should go back to her car, back home, where the man-not man might be waiting, where the sign and signaler are together, she shouldn't have to look further into the stars, when the stars are pitted deep inside of her already, lighting up like seeds in a bed in spring, unfurling their fresh sprouts and pushing through pebbles and clumps of clay to reach the sunlight.

Diana presses her back into the dry grass and imagines a stream of light underneath her body, as defined as a shadow in full sun, extending downwards, punching a perfect copy of her silhouette through the center of the earth, blasting out the other side. She is a ribbon of liquid gold and is signaling fiercely. And the humming of the man-not man begins to thread itself through her, and she knows she's made contact. Radio, on.

When she arrives the house, the lights are all out. It's not so late, is it? She quietly closes the door to the carport, hangs her keys on the nail. And he's there, standing in the kitchen, a smoky figuration in front of the refrigerator, its door open and the light shining through him in some places, other areas are more opaque, like molecules rearranging. Condensation is running in rivulets down the front of the freezer door. He stands still in a widening pool over the linoleum. She keeps her eyes on him, lowers her purse from her shoulder to the floor. The refrigerator light goes out. What did it say in the contact manual? Diana doesn't remember. So she whispers her intention, whatever my body directs me to do, I promise to follow. She feels a tiny circle of warmth at her sternum, just under the Agoudal pendant hanging from a silver chain. Diana holds the stone out from her chest as it seems to heat up, or freeze, a burning touch in the center of her palm, as she offers it to the man-not man, is it what he wants? But she doesn't understand. Of everything she can offer, it's her pendant?

A few steps forward, her whole body is being drawn into the dark corner of the kitchen. The compressor jerks on and the smell of vegetables packed too close rises up from the heated air below the fridge. The air is thick like oil. The agoudal has become unbearable against her open palm and she is afraid to see its soft shape in the dark. A pulse of white as a car passes.

And then it stops. The stone is gone from her hand. She is left with the sterling chain, and rawness in her hand. The fridge light snaps back on. This little 12W light blazes across the kitchen, the drooping produce and the softened milk cartons are illuminated like a fine painting, a still life, glowing gold and easing into decay. Diana shuts the door gently, and wipes her wet soles on the carpet when she gets to the bedroom.

The next morning, there is a note in the kitchen, a bright orange post it, stuck to the side of the fridge:

I'm sick of your collective shit.

An arrow had been drawn, with a bold black sharpie, pointing to the garbage can, which is stuffed with wilted kale and cauliflower, the cream florets tinged with black. A handful of yellowed scallions, slick at the ends. The heat still blowing full force from under the fridge. A window thrown wide open, and the smoky, residual edge of the fires lacing the dawn.

The puddle had grown and pulled out thin clumpy swirls of hair and dust from under the fridge, materials that have been gathering since they first moved in. What a disaster, Diana thinks.

Diana is at work, counting the minutes until she will leave, until she can exit this zone of the mundane, the dull, unrelenting ticking as the day passes. The words. She is so sick of the words she must use. *Absolutely. I can do that for you. Of course. It's understandable that you would. Clearly. Is there anything else I can help you with?* The efficient vocabulary of assent, bright with promises, buzzing with optimism, productivity, feels like bees in her mouth.

Someone she detests walks by. The sound of her loafers scuffing across the low pile carpeting sends a shot of adrenaline through Diana. She furtively reaches for an amethyst from her mini gem collection, a little grouping of thought-positive minerals, carefully placed in a circle where she can access them easily. She closes her fingers over the jagged, cool surface, takes a breath, and tries to release those feelings in the exhale. She closes her eyes, only briefly; she doesn't want to get caught with her eyes closed. She's afraid she might reveal something untoward in her posture, when she can't see her body. She can easily see the shoes in her mind's eye, however, their matte taupe leather, stitched up like a wound. If only she could will them away, instead of calling them closer. The woman's perfume. Diana composes an email to HR, again, pleading to disallow perfume in the office. A migraine begins to swell.

In her car, she is calm. In her car, she can breathe fresh air.

She is relieved to pass through town, is comforted by seeing everyone out, people doing everyday things. The sun beaming, an unusually clear afternoon. The shops mostly open, inside, customers bending in nutation to the sparkly lights and skillfully displayed goods. Stopped at the intersection, she looks through the open door to an ice cream counter, illuminated under a thick curvature of glass, two rows of abundant, swirling colors. There is a free parking space right in front. She pulls in, the opportunity too good to pass by. As she steps lightly onto the curb, something catches her eye. A little troll doll tied to a car antenna, its fiery orange hair still orange, but its body faded to an anemic yellow.

That must be Jason's car, but it can't be, she thinks. Of course he's working such long hours, it's possible he went out for ice cream, just like her, on a whim. The farmhouse can be lonely sometimes, it's old, so many people have lived there and gone on, their absence creeps up on you, hollows out a warm corner with a gusty draft. Diana thinks of her room again, how lovely it is, how it seems not to share the evasiveness of the house. Her plants thrive in the window, little succulents in pebbles and a few rows of African violets. Maybe Jason should put his desk in there? She feels a rush of blood to her brain, an idea, a new way forward. She is excited to share this with him. It's already clear in her mind where the desk could be situated, and maybe adding a mirror to direct the light around the room, add movement and energy. Then he wouldn't have to contend with the roommate.

As she approaches Jason's car, the reverse lights flash on, and it begins to pull out, she can't be sure but it seems like there are two people in the car. The glare of the bright blue sky, obscures the view inside, like someone threw a sheet over the back window. As the car peals out, she sees a flash of a small hand flicking a cigarette out the window. A dainty arm, like a doll's, suntanned and ringed with thin gold bracelets. A small puff of smoke from under the back wheel which is spinning, dragging rubber across the asphalt. A terrible smell lingers, that sharp burning tires in the woods smell.

People pause, turn their heads, and then resume what they were doing. The holy slow development of a shared awareness, the woman scooping bright blue ice cream, the couple holding their paper coffee cups, breaks their gaze.

This fermata of experience shared by everyone, suddenly ignites Diana. A cleared pathway through collective presence! She knows that she could harness the same power, in the group she would start, as they look out from their immediate experience, and everyone, all at once, focusing on the same thing, at the same exact time. She couldn't believe that it hadn't come to her sooner. Diana reframes the incident. Maybe it wasn't Jason after all. Most likely it was an invitation, an instructive! Like a bell chimes to begin something new.

Diana has hope. This moment, carries her high, into the ice cream shop. Well, that and her checkbook's disappearance. Would it be returned to her? Probably not. Such things must have such little importance to higher beings. A ruffle of worn papers, carefully written numbers in black ink, names and reasons for paying them. It didn't matter. But it did matter that they'd let her go, and not noticed she'd left it. A piece of evidence of her existence, something she had touched with her fingers daily. It did matter, that she'd also been asked, and examined. Her body knew. Her physical body was much more sensitive to their call, to the man-not man in her home, she just couldn't figure it out though, was he one of them, or one of her?

Sheila R. from Petaluma just purchased a Triple Light Wave blocker.
Katrina B. from Long Beach just purchased a Follow Your Body's Call Guide.
Diana M. from Santa Rosa just purchased an Agoudal pendant and ring.

The phone rings. It's Diana's mother. She doesn't usually call this early in the morning. Diana closes her laptop and puts away her credit card before answering.

Your father is really dying. You should go, Diana.

Diana pictures her mother on the phone, sitting in the tidy little vestibule by the kitchen table. The white walls unblemished, all surfaces immaculate. The Arizona heat kept at bay without any visual evidence of ducting, the advanced system's nearly silent hum and perfectly maintained temperature at 63 degrees Fahrenheit year-round. She is probably wearing a sweater, a light cardigan, cashmere. She probably still uses perfume that is better suited for baking pastries, notes of clove, vanilla, almond, rather than for one's body. Most likely there's a glass of sherry on the table.

Why should I go now if I haven't been in years? He won't even recognize me.

You know the answer to that Diana, her mom exhales and she can practically taste it. Probably still smoking 100s, as her own mother did, the longer cigarette useful for extended telephone conversations, also conducive to raising children, constantly having to pinch the half-smoked cigarette into the grooved holders in the ashtray. To break up a fight, to carry a child to the bathroom, to retrieve a fresh pair of pants, underwear.

Besides, her mother says dismissively, he probably doesn't even remember why he hasn't seen you in so long.

Diana remembers and all the times she forgot, she remembers. Her mother's face hidden in her hands, one eye puffed closed, dots of blood staining her pressed work shirt. Her father turning to look at Diana, lifting the handset from the wall, her father driving towards her and hitting the phone out of her hand, grabbing the back of her shirt as she tried to run. He never hit her, he used to remind her, and her mother's echo, you know he'd never hurt you.

Diana hangs up midsentence. She is drawn back into his house, his rooms, is afraid of what she could do when he is vulnerable, his muscles atrophied, the vigor released back into the universe. But the rage, she'd bet her life on it, remains at a blaze like the sun's explosions in the indifferent air of space. Diana knows she wouldn't try. What could it change? He's just another old man dying in the world. With any luck, he'll hurry up and go before her plane even lands. Still, she can feel the softness of a pillow in her fists and her muscles' tremor, as if she might.

The house front is unlit, save for the lights that dot the concrete path to the porch. Two rectangular glass panels on either side of the door allow a partial view inside. A circle of lamplight illuminates the hall. An enormous purse has been set on the console table by the front door, bulging against the wall, casting a lumpy shadow onto the floor, its brass hardware and chain straps gleaming.

Spotlights mounted high above the garage flood the front yard with icy light, motion detected. Diana loses her bearings, waits for her eyes to reassemble the steps up the porch, waits for the faint orange glow of the doorbell to reappear in the dark. A current of cooler air rushes in, swaying the tops of the pines. A wash of needles drifts to the ground. It seems unforgivingly isolated, at the end of the cul-de-sac. What few lamps are on, across the street, beam through the bare trunks of the pines, shooting defined blocks of light amplified by low lying fog. Diana raises her eyes to the night, the sky a soft woolly cover, suffused with orange, illuminated from the next town. No visible stars. Silent radio. She could use some help here.

The door unlocks and Diana opens her eyes. The nurse is there.

Diana, she says, wondering.

Yes, I'm Diana. It's been a while.

The nurse leans back slightly, her white sneakers in place, and flicks on the porch light, then steps aside, holding the door. Diana wants everything but this moment right now. The nurse has soundlessly shut the door and is whispering to Diana, but she is slow to hear it. A gentle line of questioning unspools from her mouth, how was the drive, the traffic, how is she feeling really, is she ok? Diana looks at the nurse's young face, wondering how many deaths had she seen, as if they could be recorded there.

She places her suitcase next to the door. She hangs her coat on the empty rack, an old wooden one, all the marks of her childhood still there. Her mother had marked her height every year with a deep notch, and now, the last recorded one etched level with her throat. She takes time removing her phone from the pockets, double checking where she put the keys to the rental, crinkling plastic ginger candy wrappers into a ball to throw away.

The rented hospital bed sits in the center of the living room, facing the sliding glass doors to a deck. If he were to open his eyes, he could see a thin strand of pines, and the small man-made lake just beyond. Diana lingers in the kitchen, searches for a glass. Waits for the water to run cold over her fingers. The nurse is leaning over the coffee table, which has been pushed right up against the low-slung couch, leaving just a small portion accessible, enough for one person to sit. She takes her phone and the can of soda.

Let me know if you need anything.

Thank you, Diana says, surprised by the meekness in her voice, as if her throat were wrapped up, muscles bound. When people are kind, she feels self-conscious, as if she should be handing something back to them, something she doesn't have.

The nurse retrieves her heavy bag from the hallway and points to the den. After she closes the door, Diana sits down, bedside. Her father lies still. She recognizes the quilt that has been laid over him, a wedding band pattern made from pink linen scraps and large cotton floral strips. There are pictures of her as a baby, struggling across the same fabric, darker in hue, straining to pull herself up, to grasp the camera, or her mother's hand. Desire sits there, lodged in the glitter of her tiny eyes, her fist squeezed tight like an unopened peony blossom.

Her father's breathing. He is turned slightly towards her. The muscles in his face have altered the structure, as if he were jutting out his chin, favoring one side for too long. His jawbone sharply visible, dry lips parted. She starts rubbing her palm with the thumb of her other hand, seeking the pressure points, relief. She doesn't know what to say, how to even begin talking. A tumble of voices come from behind the den's closed door. Laughter. The volume goes down.

The last sense to go is the hearing, her mother had said, so talk to him. You won't get interrupted, that's for sure.

Instead, Diana is tracking a fluttering moth and her eyes can't move as quickly. It settles violently against the lamp so she tries to cup it in her hands, to take it outside. It escapes and lands on top of the blanket, wings pressed flat, as though it had been painted on the quilt.

As his body shifts under the carefully spread cloth, the moth stays put. Brown and black zigzags across its wings, a thread of white dots at the edge. Diana moves cautiously, reaching her curled hands out, as if she were already holding something fragile. Her fingernails press gently at the blanket as she tries to lift only the body of the moth, not to disturb the dusty protective layer on its wings.

She flinches as her father suddenly attempts to speak, emitting a low crumbly moan. His jaw continues moving and the lips not touching, and the smell of his breath souring the air between them. His eyes are the clear, same blue of his younger self, shining. Pupils sharp as knife points.

He forms a string of sounds that lift her further out of her seat, out of necessity to hear, leaning far forward, turning her ear to him, to make sense of the thick, damp warmth of his breath, labored, and beginning to sound like a rusty whistle as he inhales.

You little cunt.

It takes Diana time to connect the meaning to sound and rather than falling backwards suddenly, she sinks in a protracted motion, until she is seated again, and a kind of searing occurs, as if looking directly into the sun, comes over her entire body. Her father's eyes remain open, fixed on Diana, and she is unable to move. Not because she is stunned, but that it just sits there, on her lap, like some rabid animal, daring her to make a move.

Gentle laughter sifts through the door. A clock strikes the time. Diana steps over to the couch, removes her shoes, and goes to sleep.

In the morning, a honking mass of geese crash into the lake, one after the other. Diana sees that the sliding door has been opened an inch; the air cuts in. She has been tucked underneath a bundle of puffy blankets. The coffee maker is hissing and gurgling in the kitchen and she can smell the first cups. She is thinking, with her eyes still closed, how much promise is contained in the brewing of coffee. How the morning hasn't been afflicted just yet, the day begins with each subsequent minute, intact.

Her father rests in the same position as last night. His breathing is even, quiet. The moth is gone.

Diana sees the nurse out on the deck, stubbing out a cigarette. She enters quietly.

Did you get some sleep?

Yes, Diana lied.

I'll be heading out soon, but you're in good hands, Jalissa is going to be with you today.

She gives Diana a tired smile as she gathers her things. Her skin is bright with moisturizer, fresh lip gloss. She looks at her watch. The doorbell rings. Diana pretends to be sleeping when Jalissa comes in. And then she pretends she is just stepping out, and drives home.

When Diana pulls into her driveway, it is almost dawn. It isn't until she gets to the front door that she realizes the whole of the house is dark. There are no other cars in the driveway but her own, the metal gently pinging and clicking as it cools. The house is silent. She flips on the kitchen light, a low buzz emits from the ceiling somewhere.

Hello?

Diana has an inexact sense that people had just left, a certain humidity indicating breath, perfume, sweat. She is disappointed, exhausted by the trip and had hoped that returning home would shake out the spindly sticks of discomfort rattling inside of her. A warm house. Jason at the computer, smiling to see her.

She drops her bag, and turns the corner into the living room. Jason's desk is tidy, the chair pushed in tight. The loveseat is gone, again, the fireplace exposed. The roommate's door is open, which makes her heart lurch—it is so unexpected. That door was never left open, only as the roommate came or went. She tiptoes over, noticing a new, small dent in the panel, torn at the edges showing splintered wood.

Hello? Her voice quavers. She stops moving, stands absolutely still to see if she can hear anything, any sign of life or threat. Nothing. Her heart swings up and she feels heat from her body, micro-currents of adrenaline charging.

She takes silent steps towards the room, flips the light switch. It doesn't work. She flips it back and forth several times. Her eyes are have adjusted to the semi-darkness enough to see that the room is empty, save for little pills of styrofoam scattered across the floor.

In her room, the bed is unmade. The tiny nightlight Jason had bought her on a work trip glows in the corner, its carved bear claw pattern glued over a piece of amber glass. As she reaches for the wall switch, the window darkens several shades and the man-not man is there; he's managed to take up more space, more light than what she remembered. He is less transparent and contains a density like a swarm, more defined, like a string drawn loosely around him.

Diana doesn't turn on the light. She closes her eyes. She imagines the stars again, and their material counterparts in her body, like magnets. Her angel is here. She lays back on the bed, feeling as though she's riding in an elevator which is plunging, stopping, plunging again. She sleeps. She remembers.

It was into a lightless room, a room with no discernible temperature. The air was thick, but not humid. It was a bright day and the clear skies unusual. She never saw the faraway earth, the perfect blue and emerald jewel that astronauts breathlessly cite, post return. She also never experienced the painful juddering of a spacecraft, the force exerted on bodies on the way to space.

Lightless rooms existing perfectly, built in time, changing as the dreamer moves through them, without ever seeing their own hands, or touching the walls. A slim doorway. A window to an unguent sea. Her body remembers that they were not rough, nor gentle, but that they approached her body with expertise. And that time, was not time, but passage, as she seamlessly went from recording numbers in a column, to the woozy awareness of the room. Object gone missing. Parts of her touched without touch and irrevocably changed, the seams and fissures of her own brain and tissues, having come together again. They'd given her a gift, the soft and generous murmuring she hears, not with her ears, but inside of her, as natural as her own blood.

She returns to her skin against the sheets, the perspiration, as it trickles minutely from her breast, trailing to under her armpit. The touch of an errant mosquito, a brushing against her. She wants to go back, where the men-not men are without language, promise nothing, but are as real as breath, pluming white in the cold morning air, and hovering.

The sun begins to rise up over the thick edge of dank morning fog, obscuring the wet lowlands and silvery leaves of eucalyptus. Her phone buzzes. The alarm for her first workshop. She had nearly forgotten. Brushing her hair into a neat ponytail, rifling drawers for a clean shirt. She sprays complexion mister all over her face, pinches her cheeks, and sits, without pants, at her little nightside table.

Diana joins the meeting. The pre-screen displays her face, her neck and the collar of her shirt. The new stone pendant is still around her neck. She touches it lightly.

Waiting for the host to let you in.

She reaches for her glasses and can suddenly see, plainly, that she is crying, that her cheeks are shining and red. The virtual doorbell chimes and a band of faces are spread across the screen like cards. She cannot pretend to hide this from anyone.

The facilitator begins.

Welcome.

She speaks from a black square, nameless, at the bottom edge.

Everyone's eyes move restlessly. The books, the shelves, the kitchens, the lights, the curtains, the coffee cups, the glasses of water, the animals drifting in and out.

Let's begin with a question. How do you know there are others like you?

Diana raises her hand first. She already knows it's a trick question.

CAROLINA / PHYLLIS GREEN

ACTIVATION OF A SLEEPER CELL POET

KAREN POPPY

If I tell the true story of how I came back to writing, no one would believe me. So trauma tells me, whispering, *You will never be believed.*

My writing pushes back against trauma, against doubts. It also celebrates its own reawakening after almost twenty years of creative silence. My writing tells me, and others: you are not alone.

For this, I give thanks to generous writers who continue to inspire me through their bravery and nurture my spirit. I have also thanked the very people who traumatized me, which must have perplexed them. Doing so also perplexed me and still does. Why should I thank them?

They did wrong, and I reacted as a hunted animal, running fast on the course of my own adrenaline, words filling pages in simultaneous action of distancing and bringing myself too close. I wrote about that too, in a poem published in my first chapbook, *Crack Open/Emergency*: "We avoid the shards, but/Some cuts are necessary./For we work close/To the pain./Closer than anybody."

In this close interaction with pain, kind human connections saved me. First, though, kind human connections gave me support to distance less from the pain.

Through it all, I wrote and wrote, and I continue to write.

As if pages could create a barrier between me and those who hurt me. As if pages could provide me with understanding of what they did to me and why. As if pages could reconcile us, we who never had a bond other than shared social circles and personal interests. I initially thought that we had the bond of mutual human decency, but given their actions, this expectation proved unfounded.

They, with power and prestige. Their feeling that they could do anything and get away with it. They laughed at me, their temporary quarry.

One day, I may write exactly what happened. It is my story to tell. The other option often holds more sway. To keep writing, as I do, and let them go to their fates. My prediction is, one will be briefly lionized and the other will become a biographical footnote. Then they will fade into oblivion. By contrast, true poets and poetry are immortal.

The wise voice says, either way, keep writing—and never rely on outcomes.

Negative Capability

Roeethyll Lunn

For me ...

I had no idea that writing was a science. I thought that it was a muse. I thought that it was some dark, phantom spirit (an Incubus) that periodically came to me in the night to wake me up and make me submit to it. I usually had to play with him until dawn. If I attempted to go back to bed, he would wake me again. He was in control and not I. I suffered his presence because I was usually satisfied with his words. I somehow had premonitions of his comings. Sometimes, he would hail me, ever so softly, in the day, in something that had filled me with awe. Or sometimes, I would hear him hiss at me through the voices of others. Having him in my life made it difficult for me to get along with others. He was my secret that they wouldn't understand, so I hid him in my daydreams. I'm in love with him. This week, in class, I found that he had a name. His name is Creativity. He is married also and has other children. Her name is Negative Capability. She shadows me during the day.

For Them ...

The term "negative capability" was penned by the poet John Keats in his "Letter to George and Thomas Keats." John Keats describes it as being "... the quality (that) formed a man of achievement , especially in literature ... (a time) when a man is capable of being in uncertainties, mysteries, doubts ...." Being in this lost condition still couldn't contain creativity. "The artist's sense of beauty," according to Keats, "overcomes every other consideration, or obliterates all consideration."

In other words, he is saying that creativity is an enigma. Some mysterious presence that takes over the behavior of its disciples, rendering them into a state of partial or full-blown insanity.

It is suggested that the artist should glory from a stance of imperfection, indecision, and doubt. He should be aware of his lack and live with it. He should allow this awareness to ostracize him into a position of an indifferent observer of mankind. The artist is then free of emotional involvement, thereby enabling him to give a true report in his art based on true insight. Negative capability, according to this, is supposedly the byproduct of creativity. Creativity is another matter. Opinions vary as to what causes creativity.

Sigmund Freud suggests that creativity grows out of a composite of all the complexes that the artist receives as a result of his having been mistreated as a child. He couples creativity with neurosis, which in turn is why the artist may be subjected to deviant behavioral patterns.

Carl Jung says in his article "The Poet" that what Freud suggests could not possibly be. Jung says:

> "The personal aspect is a limitation ... when a form of 'art' is primarily personal, it deserves to be treated as a neurosis .... What is essential in a work of art is that it should rise far above the realm of the personal life and speak from the spirit and heart of the poet as man to the spirit, the 'collective spirit,' and heart of mankind."

Creativity, Jung goes on to suggest, is God sent. God chose the artist to be a "collective man—one who carries and shapes the unconscious, physic of mankind ... he is a 'clinician,' healer, teacher and guide." In his "Letter to George and Thomas Keats," John Keats attempts to ridicule his peer for being egotistical, "...seeming not aware that his audience could see that some of the 'Poppycock,' had rubbed off on him."

In conclusion ...

The artist is a "clinician," healer, teacher and guide? Umph! I can agree with that. Even when both Jung and Freud agree that, artists, without exception, are "narcissistic ... undeveloped persons with infantile and auto erotic traits." I can agree with that ... hence Negative Capability. Although art is wearisome, isolating, and sometimes can lead to deviant behavior—like having to settle for just looking out of a window and sacrificing a beautiful day, instead of going out into it—artists continue to behave as if they have a condition that is equivalent to what drug addicts have called "a monkey on my back" or, in the case of artists, a word on their backs. I can agree with all of the theorists I've mentioned except Freud's. Freud's view is too harsh, in my opinion. I don't believe that all artists suffered from parental mistreatment, just like I don't think a person will necessarily grow up to be a serial killer just because his mother stopped him from eating his own dung. Every view had some merit, but none could actually put a finger on it. No one knows what really creates an artist, but they all agree (and I can agree with them) that an artist has problems.

John Cheeves sums it perfectly for me in his work "Good-bye My Brother." Cheeves describes how it feels to have a family member that just can't quite "fit in" in life. He says, "Oh what can you do with a man like that? ... How can you dissuade his eyes in a crowd from seeking out the cheek with acne, the infirmed hand." Umph!

Southampton, New York

1999

COUNTING / MARTHA CLARKSON

We Haven't Eaten

Christopher Bowen

We bought the house on a quiet street like a deep sigh. Children played kickball. There was a sign that said *slow down.*

She planted the rose bed first and over the years put fish bones and bone powder at each of their bases.

"The calcium helps them grow," she said, holding a flower by the stem so as not to prick herself.

She puts down a fish, an offering, at the boneyard.

We haven't eaten fish in a hundred and eighty-five days. She puts the bones over the deep, dark mulch in early fall and I have no idea where they ever come from.

I don't love her anymore, but sometimes when she says she's about to go, she kisses me on the cheek and I miss the woman she was more than when she's even around.

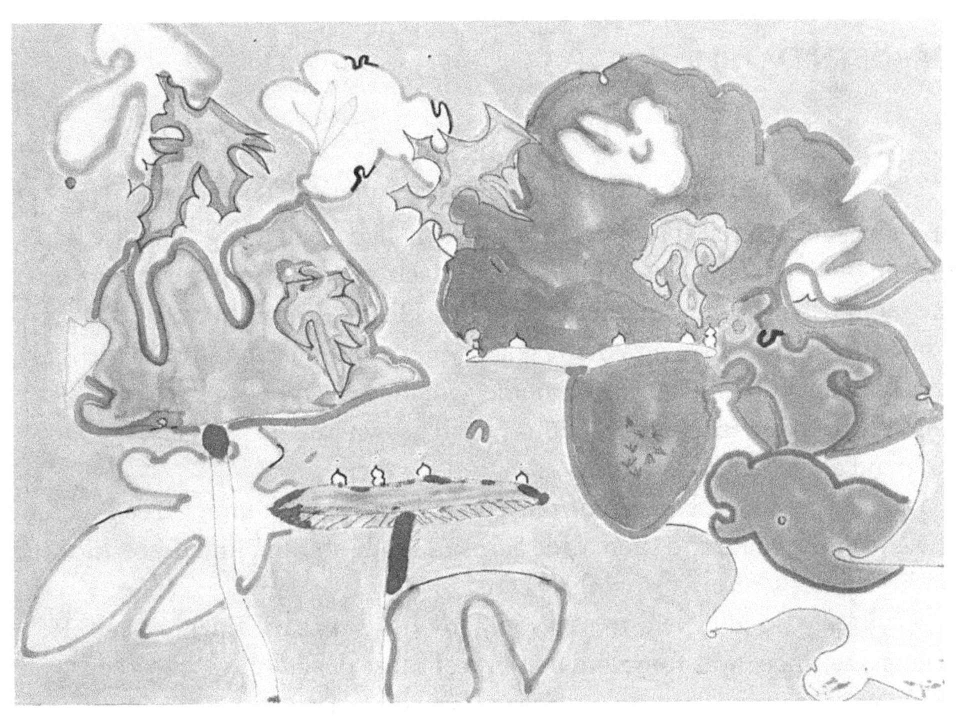

Counting on Neighbors with Cheerios / Valyntina Grenier

Reading Group A

Carolyn Dasher

It's a perfect day for work. The warm breeze smells like gardenias. The sun and surf and rocks at Moloa'a Beach look like something out of a kid's drawing—vivid yellow, deep blue, glossy black, straight from the crayon box. My mom used to bring me here when I was little. I'd splash in the shallows while she chatted up men. When I got older— when the men started furtively checking me out—she left me at home, which was a relief to both of us. And possibly to the skeezy men, too. But I'm all grown up now, and always happy to spend a morning at Moloa'a.

To get to the beach, you park on the street, duck under tree limbs at the end of the road, and then wade across a sandy stream. And there, kicking off his flipflops before crossing, is Len.

"Hey, kiddo. Nice to see you." It's never skeezy hugging Len. He's known me since I was four, and he's one of those decent guys who keeps you four in his heart forever, even once you've gotten tits.

"How's your mom?"

I tell him she's good. That she's hostessing at the new place in Princeville, and though he surely already knows this, he says, "Yeah? That's so great."

We detour around a pale, fresh-off-the-plane family setting up their beach chairs.

Len and my mom used to date. He's what my mom calls a trusty. Lucky ducky trust fund fucky. Not that you can tell by looking at him. His board shorts are ancient. His t-shirt is more holes than shirt. He buys his flipflops at Costco just like the rest of us. His tan is a deep mahogany and his hair is a little too long, these days, for his age. He's here for his morning swim. He'll take another one in the afternoon. Then he'll head out for dinner. Maybe with a woman, maybe not. He and Mom were together a long time.

Long enough that he bought me several expensive birthday presents. Long enough that no one could blame me for thinking he'd be around forever.

But Mom understood he was temporary. She kept her eyes and her options open. After a few years, he just became . . . scarce. I mean, it's impossible to avoid anyone on this island, but we somehow did not run into Len for about six months. And when we finally did see him, it was all friendly hugs and we'll have to catch up sometime, meaning not really, but hey, we're both okay and c'est la vie.

"New renters in that one," Len points up the beach toward a house with an emerald lawn and an expensively-furnished lanai. A line of palms studs the boundary between grass and sand. "Young family. Husband plays a lot of golf. Wife takes Pilates. I guess there's a nanny or something." Len lives nearby, and he has a keen eye for these things. And he knows—but is kind enough not to mention—why I'm here.

He ditches the ratty t-shirt and launches into the water. The guidebooks say you shouldn't swim at this beach. But Len could swim pretty much anywhere in pretty much any weather. When he was with my mom, he taught me how to swim and how to catch a wave, and he never once made me feel like I was in his way.

I head up the beach to the house he pointed out, snap open my straw mat, and start my routine.

Typically, they don't come out to chat on the first day. The first day is just for show. You should avoid even glancing at the house. You won't see anything in the windows but a reflection of palms and ocean. But you can sense when someone is watching. If you're lucky, it's not the wife or kids.

Focus on the routine. The stretching and twisting and balancing. You are strong and flexible and steady. The routine shows you off in all the best ways. When you're done, you sit on your beach mat, tailor style, watch the waves and emanate a sense of peace.

It's important not to appear agitated. No scratching. No fidgeting. No brushing off sand. Project a sense of dignity and calm. These men are on vacation. They're not looking for drama. Calm signals discretion. Which is one of many things they find appealing.

I calmly shift my gaze up the beach, and see that Len is out of the water now. He's lying down next to a couple of women. Younger than he is.

Len has no towel, so he's soaking theirs, but he wouldn't think about that. It's warm. The towel will dry, as will Len.

I squint to make out who the women are. One of them is Kimbra, I'm almost positive. We were at school together. She's another trusty. Actually, the child of trusties, which, depending on the family investment strategy, is just as good. Her parents didn't like the private Christian school on the island, so she attended public school with the rest of us. We were never exactly friends, me and Kimbra, but we were thrown together a lot in school, starting with Mrs. Matsui's Reading Group A.

No fish, no fruit, no animal names or colors for Mrs. Matsui, when it came to labeling her reading groups. She didn't see the point. As if we wouldn't have figured out that a particular fish was the best one, or a particular fruit the saddest and most loser-ish.

If she put you in Reading Group A, that meant that instead of the big reader with a rainbow on the cover and twenty years of student names inscribed inside, you read actual books. Books with chapters. *A Wrinkle in Time*. *Watership Down*. Instead of taking turns reading out loud, you took the books home and read them on your own. Then you discussed them with Mrs. Matsui.

Reading Group A was whispered about in the lower grades, and yearned for openly in the middle grades, by parents and students alike. But not by my mom. "There's a library," she said. "If you want to read those books, you can read those books." Which was true, but not the point. The point—which other parents understood—was to be in Reading Group A, whether you cared about the books or not. Reading Group A kids went on to take honors classes in high school. They were almost exclusively haole, Japanese or Chinese—so I had that going for me. But they were also almost exclusively kids whose clothes did not come from the Salvation Army in Kapa'a. Kids who did not live crooked stilt houses shrouded with blue tarps to keep out the rain.

My mom may not have cared, but I did. I cared tremendously about getting into Reading Group A. Which meant that all through fourth grade I was on my best behavior, turned in every assignment on time, aced all my spelling tests, practiced my handwriting until it was textbook perfect. When

Mrs. Matsui gave us quizzes at the start of fifth grade—just to "see where everyone is at"—I had to leave the room to throw up before each one.

Then one morning she sat at the reading table pressing her hands against the sides of a stack of paperbacks until each copy of *The Island of the Blue Dolphins* was perfectly aligned with the one beneath it. Before I could raise my hand to go throw up again, she called my name. She called me first, even though my last name starts with P. Then she called Kimbra, and Kiri, and Donald, and Hanna, and Linus, and Chuey.

I loved the naked envy on the faces of the kids who hadn't been called, and the horror on their parents' faces when they heard I had been. That was enough, at first. But then came the books and the questions Mrs. Matsui asked about the books. And the way she wanted us to disagree with her and with each other. I never loved anything about school as much as I loved Reading Group A.

Everyone in Reading Group A went to college except for Kiri, who got pregnant senior year and went straight to work at Big Save, and me. I made some noise about community college, but mom was getting older, and her golf course guy hadn't made the scene yet, and our meals had become mostly ramen or rice with little bits of this and that tossed in.

We needed money, and I knew how to get it. So I did.

Now Mrs. Matsui, when she runs into me at Big Save, looks past me into the distance, as if we never had those amazing conversations about Captain Nemo or *The House of Dies Drear*.

Kiri and I have stayed close. Most of the others got jobs in Honolulu or on the mainland after college—I see them around at Christmas time. We wave and smile. Kimbra got her degree and came back. She waves and smiles, too. She throws terrific parties, or so I hear. Kiri gets invited, but not me.

Kimbra works as PA for some celebrity with a house in Kilauea. Which means when the celebrity's arrival is imminent, she stocks the kitchen, makes sure the Range Rover is tuned up and the tank is full, orders the flowers, confirms that the sheets and towels and things I probably can't even imagine are all fresh and ready. She schedules the airport pickup, the golf rounds, the massages and spa treatments. And when the celebrity leaves, Kimbra makes sure the fridge is empty, the Range Rover is tarped, the pool is covered, the house cleaned, the lanai furniture cushions stored away. She doesn't do these things herself, I've been made to understand. She coordinates the doing of them by others. For this coordination, according to Kiri, she gets paid a shocking amount of money.

Good for her. She's smart to earn. My mom's grandparents came here from the mainland with money to burn. And they burned every dollar. They built two houses. Because they were not imaginative people, they called the inland one Mauka (mountain) and the beachfront one Makai (ocean). When their inheritance dwindled, mom's parents sold Makai. So now there's just Mauka. The roof leaks. The stilts on the weather side are slowly rotting. The house kneels toward the ocean, like it's bowing toward a distant Polynesian ancestor. Some wet season not too far in the future it will probably keel right over.

Paradise, it turns out, is perpetually damp, mildewy and full of dry rot. But in the beautiful house behind me, and in the house Kimbra manages, the sheets are always dry and crisp. The towels smell as fresh as spring meadows.

I stand—no hands, because I can gracefully rise from the ground without them—and roll up my beach mat.

You never carry a beach chair. Not just because they're expensive—the good ones—but because you are not a pack horse. And because a chair hides your body, which entirely defeats the purpose of you being here, in front of this fancy house. No towel, because towels fill up with sand which must be shaken out—a matronly action that evokes scolding children for tracking dirt through the house. Your straw mat sheds sand the second you lift it off the ground. You bend at the waist as you roll it up and let whoever is watching get a good look at your lovely ass. You tuck the roll under your arm and amble up the beach as if you have all the time in the world. Which you do.

If you felt someone watching, you come back the next day— same time—and do it all again.

That's usually when he'll come out. Ask if you're "native." This is not the moment for a history lesson. There are shockingly few natives left on these islands, but these men don't come here to learn about things like that.

I have dark hair and a year-round tan, but I am completely haole. Any local would never think otherwise. No going into that. All he means is did I grow up here. "I grew up right down the road," I lie. My mom couldn't have afforded anything near this beach. But I spent plenty of time at Len's, and I gesture vaguely in the direction of his house.

"Beautiful," he says. Which could mean the place, or which could mean me. And that's when I know I'm in.

A few days later he informs me that his wife and kids have left for Maui—her parents have a condo there. He's hanging back though. He needs the quiet for a deal he's working on.

You never ask questions about the deal. A: you're supposed to be a break from their routine. B: they're sure you couldn't understand it. When they're sure about something, they're happy, which is how you want them. A happy man, even if his happiness is an illusion, is a generous man.

A wife in Maui means expensive dinners out. It means modeling dresses and bikinis for him at the boutiques in Princeville. It means scrambled eggs—they are all so proud of their scrambled eggs; an egg is just an egg, but you can ooh and aah with the best of them —and coffee on the lanai. It means you can use the classes left on his wife's Pilates punch card if you want.

There will be gifts. Gifts are the point. This is mutually understood. Express your gratitude but don't act too blown away. Make him feel good when he gives you things, but never let him see your need. Needing is not sexy. Needing is messy. Thank him in a calm, low voice. Slowly extend your hand, angled to accent the delicacy of your wrist, and accept the offering of the moment. Bring the gift gracefully to your lips, your heart, wherever it is you'd like him to direct his gaze.

I tuck the punch card into my waistband—watch his eyes follow it as I take another sip of coffee. He's golfing later, he says, so maybe I could take a class then. "Sure," I say. "I'll do that." They like to keep you occupied. They don't want you at loose ends, stretching and twisting on some other beach in front of some other guy's rental.

Some gifts can be exchanged for cash later. Others must be used as intended. I put on my best gear and go to the Pilates class. The woman at the desk scrutinizes the card and its star-shaped punches. "I don't remember you," she says, "and I remember everyone who comes here." She's the little sister of someone I went to high school with—I actually do remember everyone—and she's not quite certain if I'm who she thinks I am.

People talk about me. The same way they used to talk about my mom. I know what they say. But I don't have a trust fund like Kimbra. And I don't want to clean vacation houses or stock shelves at Big Save. Or rent out snorkel gear. Or any of that shit. I want to go the beach and eat nice meals and enjoy eggs and coffee on fancy lanais. I want to try on pretty dresses and have someone else pay for them. I want to be touched by men who think my body and my skin are amazing, who make worshipful noises as I slide between their crisp, dry rental house sheets.

This life comes with an expiration date. My mom is a restaurant hostess now, and she goes home to a boyfriend who mows the greens on the golf course. He's nice. She's happy. "I got it all out of my system when I was young," she likes to say. Also: "Why would you settle down unless you didn't have a choice?"

The receptionist's fingertips go white, she's pinching the card so firmly. Like I might snatch it back from her. I shrug. "My friend went to Maui, and she had some classes left. But if it's a problem . . ." She punches another star in the card and reluctantly releases it back to me.

I've taken Pilates classes before. I incorporate the more attractive moves into my beach routine. In flush moments, I've paid my own way. But usually a guy treats me. The other women in the studio can tell—like it's a scent I give off—that I don't really belong there. They shift their mats away from mine, wary.

That night my mom seats the two of us at one of the better tables in her restaurant. She talks up the specials, tells him they're running low on the seared tuna—this is her way of letting me know she'll save me one. She unfolds his napkin and offers him a long look at her cleavage as she drapes it across his lap. After the seared tuna comes a shared dessert—only a tiny bite for me, thanks—and a final scotch for him. Then Mom slides the bill in front of him. She turns and winks at me, the only moment of recognition between us. Even our waitress, who's known me all my life, doesn't give me away. But she'll be talking in the kitchen when she thinks my mom can't hear. "It's such a shame," she'll say. "She was so smart in school."

That night you have another drink back at his rental, and then a couple more. He puts on music and you dance. He's a good dancer. You never expect it with these guys, but they occasionally surprise you. He knows where to put his hands and how to guide you into a rhythm and before long you are on the fluffy rug in the living room, and he's taking off your top, and the drink is swirling in your head, and he says, "I just want to feel you. Really feel you." And you want to really feel him, too, so you say yes. Yes to everything. And it's great. It's the best you've had in a long time. And since he's leaving soon, you let him know that it's the best you've had in a long time. And this is a mistake, because when you say your final goodbyes, there's no gift card, no special piece of jewelry, no little something to remember him by. He thinks he's already given you the gift of a lifetime.

Which, it turns out, he has.

The responsible thing to do is get a test. I'm in the parking lot at Big Save by seven a.m., right when it opens. But there's Kiri, dodging puddles as she runs for the door. She sees me and waves, opens her eyes wide at me as if to say, "Rain!" and "What are you doing here so early in the morning?"

I wiggle my phone at her, my eyes saying back, "Yeah, I know," and "Oops. Gotta go."

I'll come back later when, hopefully, someone else is working the till.

The swell is up, and Kiri's such a surf ho, I was sure she'd drop the kids with her mom and call in sick. But you can only do that so often. I briefly consider heading to Foodville, but Foodville means tourist prices, and I can't float that this month. I can't even float enough gas to drive down to the Safeway in Kapa'a. Which would be the best place. Although even there, I'd probably see someone I know.

Subtract out the tourists and it's a small island—all of us up in each other's business.

Where can I go on my last gallon of gas? What will I do with myself today? It's a Saturday—turnover day—so pickings will be slim. But you never know. No point in doing my beach routine until people are up and about though. Maybe Jillia will share the bounty from whatever house she's cleaning. But checkout's not til 10 or 11, so I've got time to kill.

Just then Paolo raps on my window. "Hey, girl, what're you doing here so early?" Paolo runs the Brazilian food cart, even though he's not

Brazilian. The food cart people start early. Really, almost everything starts early here, so he shouldn't be surprised to see me. Everyone's trying to catch a wave or get in a swim before work. I do these things too, even though I don't exactly keep standard hours. Work starts when I want it to start. Sometimes it starts while I'm out for a morning jog around the golf course, dressed in my best Lululemons and my too-revealing-to-be-supportive sports bra.

"You hungry?" asks Paolo. And yes, I realize I am. He fries me some plantains. I dip into my precious cash to treat him to a coffee from one of the other carts. "No coffee for you?" he asks. I lie and tell him I've had my daily quota.

Later, I sit at a breakfast bar watching Jillia empty out the refrigerator in her first house of the day. "You need any mustard?"

If you know someone who cleans rentals, you never have to buy mustard or ketchup—there's an endless supply of barely touched bottles free for the taking. Also the dregs of chip bags and cereal boxes, of liquor and wine bottles. Partial six-packs of soda and beer, half limes and half lemons, and hit-or-miss containers of take out. I'm not proud —if it smells okay, I'll happily eat it. Usually. But lately, I confess to Jillia, nothing smells good. Lately I'm having trouble keeping down even the blandest food. Just the smell of scrambled eggs and coffee would have me puking over the edge of the most beautiful lanai.

"I thought you had an implant," says Jillia. She was the sharpest girl in my grade. Not the best student, not Reading Group A material, but she never misses a trick. "Paolo said you were at Big Save bright and early this morning, but you didn't go in. He said you looked off, and he's right."

So this is what they'll all be talking about now. Like mother, like daughter. My mom got knocked up when she was twenty-one. And here I am, perilously close to thirty, more than old enough to know better, following in her footsteps. I sometimes wonder when my expiration date will kick in, and today I think it's more likely a matter of months than years. Maybe I should start applying for restaurant jobs. Maybe I should ask Mom's boyfriend if he has any younger friends on the greens crew.

"It's pretty old," I say, probing the ridge beneath my skin. "I've been meaning to get it taken out."

Jillia drops a half loaf of bread and a stick of butter into her cooler and puts her hands on her hips. "Well, girl, what now?"

I sigh and push the takeout container further down the breakfast bar, away from my sensitive nose.

"You should talk to Kimbra."

I laugh. I haven't talked to Kimbra in years.

"Seriously. Kimbra knows how to hook things up."

I shake my head. I know how to hook things up myself. I've done it before, and pretty much assumed I'd need to do it again someday, seeing as I'm lax about things like replacing my implant. "I'm keeping it," I say. Out loud and to someone else, so it must be true.

Jillia doesn't respond. Maybe she disapproves. Or maybe she simply has to keep moving, keep cleaning. She has another house to clear by 4 pm. The most time-consuming thing is the laundry. The dryer buzzes. "I'll get it," I say. I start the towels and put clean sheets on a bed, and prepare to explain that I want to be a mom, and I know how do my job and raise a kid. My mom did just fine by me, after all. And I'll do even better. If my kid wants to be in Reading Group A, or whatever, I'll help her make that happen. But Jillia isn't looking for an explanation. I return just as she finishes mopping the kitchen, and, as if no time has passed, she says, "I thought you might. All the more reason to talk to Kimbra."

"For what? Advice about having a kid?" Kimbra is single and childless and has never shown much interest in me.

But Len has. I flash to the two of them, lying on her wet towel at Moloa'a. Talking intently. About me?

Jillia shrugs as if it's not her place to say, and I decide I'd rather catch some waves than watch her vacuum the carpets.

The swell has died and the waves are shitty, but I do my best. When I get back to my car and fish my phone out of the glove compartment, there's a message from Mom. "Hi honey. I ran into Kimbra yesterday. She wants to talk to you."

Absurd. The last time Kimbra talked to me was shortly after graduation when she gave me some lame excuse for not inviting me to her summer luau. But we both knew the real reason why. I was already in the game.

"I'm expanding," Kimbra says. She finally called me directly and invited me to lunch, which means I've joined her at the picnic table in front of Paolo's food cart. "Referrals," she spirals her fork in the air, indicating skyrocketing demand for her services. She needs someone to help her manifest the many luxuries that must be manifested whenever one of her clients aims a private jet toward our little island. That someone must be reliable, discreet, and smart.

"Len suggested you. And I thought, right! Reading Group A!" She holds out a fist and I obligingly bump it with my own. When I don't lunge at her offer (needing isn't sexy, needing is messy), she stifles her surprise and gives me a week to think about it.

A day later she calls and tells me the job will, naturally, come with an array of benefits, including, should I ever need it, maternity leave.

Two days later, Mom calls and talks about how much it would mean to her if we could afford to fix up Mauka. How, if I didn't want to live there myself anymore, we could rent it out. Have Jillia manage it.

Three days later, Len calls. "Take the job, kiddo," he says. "It's the right play."

Everyone on the island is in on it. They're blocking all the other exits and channeling me toward this single remaining door, which might as well have "Opportunity" painted on it in neon letters. Once I walk through it, they can all applaud Kimbra for rescuing me.

I inspect myself in the mirror every morning. I'm not showing yet, but for the last two weeks my beach routines have landed zilch.

Mrs. Matsui used to tell us to make the most of our opportunities. She assumed that Reading Group A was just the first of many that would come our way.

Opportunities don't always look the way you think they will. Also, you can't eat pride. So I call Kimbra and say yes. She offers a salary which surpasses my expectations, but for form's sake, and because I'm not an idiot, I counter with a higher number, to which she agrees. Then she says she's putting the signing bonus (the signing bonus!) in the mail right away.

I walk around Mauka wondering how much mold lurks beneath the carpets—those will all have to be pulled up—and what it will cost to replace the stilts and repair the roof. When the signing bonus arrives, I pay all the bills with red "final notice" stamps on them and then decide it's time to buy that test and confirm what I already know to be true.

On my way out of Big Save, my test safely hidden in a brown paper bag, I run into Mrs. Matsui. She has her canvas shopping totes slung over one arm, and she casts a disapproving glance at my paper bag. Behind her, her very fit, handsome son is asking do they need a cart. Eric, I remember. He was a senior when I was a freshman. More of a jock than an Honors English kind of guy — possibly just to push his mother's buttons. He's recently back from the mainland, where he did something in tech. According to Paolo, he took a big payout and now he's home. Consulting. Which, since you can do it from anywhere, why not from paradise?

A family of tourists dithers in the store entrance. The rest of us, who need to be particular places at particular times, roll our eyes at one another and edge past them. The gap for edging past is narrow, which means Mrs. Matsui must either speak to me or make a show of being rude to me.

"Well, look who it is. I'm so pleased to see you," she says. All smiles. Her son is all smiles, too, behind her, where she can't see him looking me up and down.

"I hear you're going to be working with Kimbra. Such a great opportunity. Reading Group A girls sticking together!"

"Yay, Reading Group A," I say with a little ironic fist pump.

Eric laughs and winks at me. Mrs. Matsui purses her lips and hurries past me into the store. Her son follows, still smiling, giving me another once-over before he joins her in the produce area. I watch for a minute. He doesn't turn around to look at me again, but that's okay. I know the closest beach to Mrs. Matsui's house. I know where to find him.

Store and Funeral Home VI

/ Christopher Paul Brown

Untitled, North Riverside Dubuque Iowa 2022

/ Christopher Paul Brown

Untitled, North Riverside Dubuque Iowa 2022

/ Christopher Paul Brown

UNTITLED, EAST DOWNTOWN

/ CHRISTOPHER PAUL BROWN

Anna in a Precarious Pose

/ Christopher Paul Brown

VALENTINE

JOANNA URBAN

On Valentine's Day, the boyfriend makes her beef bourguignon and presents her with a scarf from his trip to Prague. In Boyfriend's studio apartment, they lie on his bed, which is next to the refrigerator and lacks a headboard. On top of mismatched sheets, they sprawl out and watch the short program of pairs figure skating on the Winter Olympics. Her eyes are glued to the ice skaters, watching the sequins shimmer on their leotards as they glide, leap, and pirouette across the slick, white ice. She starts crying, which bewilders Boyfriend. Did I do something wrong? he asks. Well, he has never traveled to Prague in the time they've been together, she thinks but doesn't say this. Of course not, she says instead, wondering what he was thinking, who he was thinking of when he purchased that scarf. Mostly, she's crying at the perfect synchronization of the skaters' bodies, how they intuit each other's next moves; she knows she doesn't have this with Boyfriend and wonders if she'll ever have it with anyone.

The next February fourteenth, her new boyfriend, a divorcé ten years her senior, surprises her with a bouquet of flowers delivered to her office. Her colleagues marvel at this display of romance. Never let this one go, they say, their voices laced with wisdom and knowing. New Boyfriend makes them a reservation at a buzzy, modish restaurant with an elaborate menu requiring extensive predinner googling. There, as their hyperlocal microgreens are being served, they run into New Boyfriend's boss who mistakes her for the ex-wife. You look so much like—the boss cut himself off. Never mind, he says, wishing them a happy Valentine's Day. New Boyfriend tries to conceal his discomfort, but the tautness of his smile, the heaviness in his eyes, give away how odd he feels.

As the weeks pass New Boyfriend's texts and calls grow less frequent. A slow drifting. Then, his inevitably gutting words: He's not ready for a serious relationship. He tells her he's sorry, but he wants to see other people. Don't lie to me, she yells, you want to see one other person! She shrieks at him like a crazy person, waving her arms in wild gestures, and it's a little bit satisfying. She has never allowed herself to be so mad at a man before.

Religiously, torturously, she stalks him and the ex-wife on Instagram. Half a year later, they're back in each other's pictures.

The year after that, she adopts a rescue puppy that first week of February. A three-month-old mutt with teeth as sharp as toothpicks that gnaw on her hands for attention. The pink pads of his paws quiver and flit while he dreams, and he squawks—a piercing birdlike chirp— when he's hungry. He tests her patience when he pees on the floor for the twentieth time, chews up a computer charger, barks at a ladybug crawling across the windowsill. On the puppy's twenty-first accident in the house at least he pees by the front door, which makes her heart soar with hope; he's making progress.

She walks him outside and he tugs at his leash, stops in the middle of the sidewalk, and sits down in protest. Neighbors pass by telling her how cute and perfect the puppy is, and she accepts their compliments like a proud mom, her frustration with him melting away.

The next winter she has a fiancé. In January, they moved into a five hundred square foot apartment together, only marginally larger than the tiny one-bedroom she's lived in since tiring of roommates. Fiancé makes her coffee and oatmeal for breakfast every morning, and he lets the grown puppy sleep at the foot of their bed. Fiancé is not boastful or showy about his love for her, but she can tell that he indeed considers himself lucky. When she leaves for a work trip, he reorganizes the kitchen cabinets over the weekend; he's bored and restless without her, and she can tell that she was missed. Fiancé is obsessed with puppy, always buying him new balls and rope toys, and organic, grain-free treats. This is wonderful, because puppy is her child, and love for puppy means love for their future with more four-legged and maybe two-legged children one day.

For Valentine's Day, he buys her gold-plated earrings from a local shop and brings flowers home to her that she trims and prunes each day. The bouquet lasts for almost a week—blooming, lingering, nourished with daily fresh water—until clumsy puppy knocks it over while jumping to steal a piece of steak.

The Age of Death

Tetman Callis

I gotcha, Dad. I gotcha.

I know it hurts, Dad. It'll be over soon.

No, Dad. No. You can't get up. I'm sorry, but you can't. If you try to get up you'll fall down and we won't be able to pick you up and get you back in bed, there's only me and Mom here and we're not strong enough.

No, Dad.

It's all right, Dad. Everything is okay, it's going to be okay.

It didn't matter what book it was. Hard to concentrate.

The time was early and the car was mostly empty.

That girl, she was very pretty. Up by the other door. She sat and focused on her phone.

Specter didn't want her to catch him looking. He didn't stare. Looked around, eyes going here and there, taking things in, watching out, the way you do in the city.

There was an angry guy in the car. Young man, maybe twenties. He muttered and cursed. The girl ignored him. But you could see she knew he was there. You could see her tense up, even from the other end of the car.

Specter kept an eye out. A wary eye, and an ear, too. What would he do if the angry young man went off? Specter was pushing sixty. He'd push the intercom button and call for help.

The angry young man got off at the next stop. Specter watched him giving forearm blows to a shelter at the stop as the train pulled away.

The girl got off two stops later. Specter missed her as soon as she was gone. He missed them all.

Illinois was farms. Missouri wooded mountains. Downtown Dallas steel and glass and bright reflections. The approach path into El Paso over low brown desert mountains—he hiked those mountains when he was young.

Cats at the motel. One in the parking lot, in the glare of headlights. Then another, and another, and more. Cats in the bushes and hedges. Furtive felines, their own society, together but apart.

Specter and his mom sit at the dining table in his mom's house. Had been his mom and dad's, now hers alone. They had been together a long time. A lifetime. He can see the loneliness.

Specter and his mom eat chicken noodle soup and share an orange. Talk of his dad's things, of money.

No, Mom. Don't give me any. I don't want it and I won't take it.

This was only half true. He did want it. But he wouldn't take it. Think of what people would say.

His parents reached the age of death. That long voyage through time that only the truly fortunate are cursed to endure. Friends and family dropping away, one by one, faster and faster.

His mom's best friend, emphysemic, smoked long white cigarettes, later was connected by a long clear tube to a wheeled tank, gone after three frantic days of telephoning family and wandering the streets.

His dad's best friend, long wheelchair-bound, body breaking down piece by piece, system by system, gone one morning after a hemorrhagic flood from the nose, bursting from within his skull.

Then his father, worn out by the decades, kidneys shutting down, liver shutting down, appetite gone, fitfully awake in pain and unquenchable thirst, sent home from the hospital to die in his own bed. Hospitals are places for those who may live. Every death in a hospital is an accidental death.

The widow is crippled in one arm and has a speech impediment. She comes to Specter's mom's house two days after Specter's dad has died, before Specter's dad has been rendered into ash and fragments.

Knock, knock.

Who's there?

The widow brings an Arby's and a Pepsi to give to Specter's mom, though Specter's mom does not eat and drink Arby's and Pepsi. And lately she hadn't been eating or drinking much at all. Her husband had been dying, suffering, it takes one's appetite away.

I came to see what you were going to do with your husband's bed. It's a good bed. Can I have it?

Specter pulls up in his rental in the space in front of his motel room. Cats scatter. Two people, a couple, man and woman, are at the door to his room, trying to get in. Specter gets out of his car.

Excuse me, but what are you doing?

They explain and it's a misunderstanding, misdirection by the desk clerk, the motel's layout is confusing.

I'm sorry, I don't know where your room is, but it is not right here.

Specter walks the neighborhood from one end to the other, wending up and down various streets. He hasn't walked it like this since he was a restless teenager, prowling on foot, looking for friendship and love. He walks by houses he hasn't walked by in over forty years. Much has changed. The cars, of course. The yards, drought and rationing have brought an end to green grass and now the yards are all stone and concrete. The people, he knows they have all changed, moved away or died. He doesn't know anyone who still lives here besides his mom and dad, now just his mom.

He stops in front of Winter's house. Stands on the sidewalk, big and bold as brass on a sunny desert day. Someone comes out? Comes out to say, What are you doing? Why are you staring at my house? But no one comes out. He almost didn't recognize the house. Its facade mostly brick, the color hasn't changed, though it's not the color he remembers. But he remembers the porch. He remembers the front door, the direction it faced. He remembers where on the block the house was at, what part of the block, which side of the street. There's only one house in this part of the block with a front door that faces that direction, so this must be the one. He remembers one night, he and Winter stood on this porch, and the things they did and said. He was sixteen and she was fourteen. They had forever.

He can't stand there forever. He turns around to look across the street. He knows Evie lived in one of those houses. He's pretty sure he knows which one. He lived there too, for a while, when he was down on his luck and Evie talked her mom into taking him in. He stayed until he wore out his welcome, and then he left.

He walks on. Block after block. There is no one out.

He reaches the block where he grew up. He walks up it. He has made this walk several times already in the years since he left, since his parents moved a few blocks away to the house his mom lives in now and his dad died in. Here, this block, when he was growing up here, no one died. He doesn't need to rifle through his memories as he walks up this block to the cross street. There are too many of them, and he has been over them over and over.

He turns left and continues. A half-block on he passes the corner where he and Tina first kissed. He stops and contemplates. He didn't remember that telephone pole.

He walks on. He is going to Tina's house. He knows she doesn't live there anymore. She left years ago, and as far as that goes, it goes all the way to the end. He knows she died a dozen years ago. He goes to her house anyway, to see it again, closer than he's been since their days together in school.

He doesn't remember the address, but he remembers the house. He stands and looks. The driveway where Tina and he made out one spring afternoon after school, hidden from view behind her father's car, unbuttoning and unfastening. The driveway now shaded by an awning, aluminum siding held up on thin poles. Beyond the drive, the window on the wall of the converted garage that was Tina's bedroom. The things they did there. Beside the driveway, between it and the house next door, the place that was grassed and cool and where he and Tina and their friends gathered to drink soft drinks and smoke cigarettes and incessantly shoot the breeze on any clement evening. It's now paved. Pure flat concrete, gray in the weak sunlight.

He walks on. Down the block and to the right and past the junior high school. They don't call them junior high schools anymore. Middle schools now. It's being torn down. Its parking lot and part of its athletic field dotted with a formation of portable classrooms, the old structure is being razed so that something new and modern can be erected in its place. No more nostalgic visits to its halls from old graduates.

He turns and heads back to his mom's house. It's a long walk. The neighborhood was new when he grew up here. Now everything looks tattered and worn. His cell phone buzzes in his pocket but he doesn't answer.

The only time he watches television anymore is in motels. He doesn't travel often. Television is so strange. The constant hectoring and manipulation. Buy this. Do that. Go here. Be concerned. Constantly there's something to concern you in all that doesn't concern you. Make it yours. Worry. Fret. Be outraged. Be afraid of lacking everything you lack.

The ceremony is this morning and he finishes getting dressed. Doesn't often have chance or call to wear a suit. Checks his look. Tie is straight.

The white limousine pulled up in front of the house. Specter and his mom walked down the driveway. Slowly, she's old.

The honor guard in the cemetery snapped to attention as the limo slowly passed.

There were friends there. Friends of his dad's and his mom's. Not many. His parents were quiet people, kept to themselves, their home, their flowers and trees and bushes and small patch of real lawn out back where the city couldn't see how often they watered.

A cloudy and chilly day. The seasonal winds already beginning. The man from the funeral home had a blanket to spread over Specter's mom's lap where she sat on the bench. The urn containing the ashes of her husband was placed on the bier. In a moment, the minister and the man from the funeral home moved it one level lower so it wouldn't be knocked over by the wind.

The honor guard folded the flag. Precisely, in careful time and with serious intent. One of the guard brought the folded flag to Specter's mom, knelt in front of her, murmured some words, presented to her the flag.

The honor guard fired the volley, the shots loud in the cold late morning. The bugler played "Taps," the notes clear and long.

There were things to go through back at the house, papers to sort.

A boxing match on television at the motel. Nothing Specter would ordinarily watch, but when you travel . . . the match went ten rounds and Specter watched them all. Thought about his dad.

Specter's dad taught him to throw a forearm blow and not to throw a punch. Taught him to do whatever it took.

Don't be afraid to pick up an equalizer.

An equalizer, Dad?

Yeah, like a two-by-four.

Specter's dad had been a sergeant, had fought in wars.

The match was a split decision. The former champ won on points. It could've gone either way.

Cats in the motel parking lot at dawn. Furtive and feline, leave us alone, this life is hard.

Breakfast at sunrise. Specter sat in a booth at the diner, ate his bacon and eggs and drank his coffee, watched while the sun illuminated the mountains, rugged and treeless peaks dusted with snow.

At the airport there were Border Patrol agents in combat fatigues, carrying automatic rifles. What invasion at the airport were they waiting for? Specter was glad he was of the race that most readily passed.

He had an aisle seat on the flight back. The seat beside him was empty, a rarity on flights. A young woman sat in the window seat, drew the shade, leaned her head to sleep. Specter stared at the pages of his book. The baby in the row ahead was quiet. There was another baby farther back in the cabin, cried a bit. Specter thought as to how we were all babies once. Every one of us, carried and coddled and cared for, every need attended to.

Hush, little baby. Don't you cry. You'll be a grown-up, by and by.

Hush, little baby. It's going to be all right. You're okay. Mommy's right here. She's okay. Daddy's waiting at home and he's okay, too.

Hush, little baby.

Caught Between

Laura Eppinger

You're invited: Small Birthday Party for Our Small Child

When: Next Saturday, 1-3 p.m. should be the warmest hours of the day.

Where: Our backyard! The other side of this invitation includes a map of the neighborhood. Just one block to steer clear of—hard to explain if you've never been here before.

We realize February is still chilly out, so we'll see how long we last! Some of you post so many selfies on airplanes or in Disney World, it's hard to believe you aren't exhaling COVID right now. Then again, we just bought a house one block away from a lethal whirlpool monster. Spouse tells me we are in no place to judge, since we just caved to the pressure of a rabid housing market.

What to bring: Just yourselves, all bundled up! We don't need gifts for the little one, really. She's never had a party beyond Spouse and me singing to her for her first and second birthdays, so she doesn't expect a spectacle. We bought far too much stuff online during lockdown. Spare us!

RE: the map on the other side of this glossy invite I also ordered online. Please plan your route ahead of time. On your Maps app, this chunk of real estate will appear as a little pond with a fountain spritzing to the sky every summer. Trust me when I say this is not an accurate description.

It is a hungry beast, sentient though it is just a water spout. No face, no eyes, no voice. The whirlpool seems to wield gravity; it will suck in your SUV and all inside, so do not even try to approach on foot. (It goes without saying, but DO NOT gift Small Child a bike!)

Is it careless to invite others to our home, knowing their minivan could be slurped off the pavement and into the gullet of an angry beast? Sure. Feel free to decline this invitation. We have almost certainly declined one of yours recently.

You can probably tell that I MISS PEOPLE. My wise friends are too cautious to hang out. My reckless friends—do you not know about my father-in-law? —talk about being so over face coverings. But before all this, we were close. You absolutely know that one of your open-mouthed coughs inside my living room could lay waste to Spouse's parents. Still. I miss your selfishness and stubbornness and rude gaping yawns.

Do I think Small Child is traumatized? Oh probably, by the stress of her parents alone. Not by pandemic restrictions, per se. Not by the wearing of masks. I know some of you hold these loopy opinions and you don't know this but I've muted you on Facebook. But not deleted. I can't because, as I said above, I miss you. Maybe one day you'll leave those deranged parenting groups? I dare to dream. It's like being caught between ... like being trapped between ... I'm so fried from the strain I can't think of a metaphor.

RSVP: Just show up, or don't. The longing for grownup conversation is unbearable though the fear of losing you to Charybdis looms large. Come to my party and risk being devoured. Stay home and let loneliness nibble away at your heart by another bite. Either way I'll be serving an excellent spiked hot chocolate I learned from a TikTok!

The Sound Cicadas Make

Garrett Candrea

There's a simple pleasure in this, childlike and dumb but also comforting, reassuring, how they sound like it says on the box: bang, snap. Sometimes pop. The minutes seem to falter, stagger, to do things such things as minutes are incapable, to ramble, some restless hour in the night when he steps out back to throw bang-snaps off the deck.

He throws them one at a time, pausing between each, thinking, call it contemplating, the little orange sparks flashing against the dark and how it doesn't matter what you call them. He removes another whiz-bang from the pack, all sawdust and cigarette paper, the feel of these between his fingers, and the other times and other places.

He'd once said to a client, Get rid of them.

They hit the driveway below making the light they make and the sound and it is otherwise quiet out here near the edge of town, wind sifting through the pines.

He'd once told the boy, or was it the son, to make a wish.

He's standing barefoot in briefs and wrinkled tee and this is not unusual but something he does when he can't sleep, when he's been roused awake by a dream that has for hours left him lying there in his sweat in the basement pullout, staring where people stare while they wait for their alarm to go off.

Brittle and soft and fine and flimsy. Call it distraction. Call it procrastination. He holds between his fingers one of the whackers, something else they're called by some other sound they make.

He remembers the last time he'd gone up to his son's room, to the door with the splintered dent that'd been punched into the wood among the Ian Lundy quotes scrawled out in black marker. He remembers the empty trash bags in his hand and how he'd gone in there intent on filling them with clothes for the needy but instead sat in his son's computer chair and placed one over his head and used his belt to cinch it shut at his throat. Whop or boom. Call it pathetic. It wasn't until he'd begun to feel faint that he'd realized that wasn't what he'd wanted to do, not like that and not at all, so panicked that his fingers fumbled with the buckle and he had to tear the bag open at his mouth, gasping for air. When he finally got the belt loose he chucked it across the room. At first he was gasping, then he was crying. Then he began to laugh, the torn bag still over his head. He was thinking of something she would have probably said, something so simple and crass but in that dry tone she liked to use—it had him gasping for air all over again and he felt crazy but at least he was aware of it—*you dumb idiot.*

For thinking that was the answer. For even having considered it. For blaming himself. These were all things his support group had said when he'd told them about what had happened, what he'd tried to do, the faces arranged in a circle and staring at him in soft reproach. It was not his fault, they'd told him. He'd done the best he could, they'd told him, these mothers and fathers sitting in a church basement who had likewise lost a child to overdose. But it was all of it just words, hollow syllables, the same boilerplate phrases they liked to exchange with each other week over week, allowing themselves to be convinced by the stock mantras. They never knew the truth of it, and he hasn't been to a session in nearly six months.

Now, on the deck, in the cool night, he shakes the rest of the whipper-snappers into his hand and chucks them over the rail. It only takes a second: the crackle and glitter of orange light.

He'd once said to the kid, It's different when you're the one doing it.

All this a dull sound somewhere.

Come morning he's sitting in the living room with the TV on while pale colors play wearily on the walls. As in things remote, things separate, aloof. There's less than an hour of sleep behind his eyes and his alarm will go off any minute now, the drowsy light gathered at the edges of the blinds tells him this, reminds him of this, of lazy times lying beside her in slatted shadows, times when they both had the day off and could waste away in easy languor while the city shifted and creaked beyond the window. How young they were then, two years out of college and living happily in a fifth-floor walkup in Queens, cast-iron radiators and a fridge that curdled milk before its expiration date. The good times always get left behind, those dusty mundane moments, how they used to stare up at the water-stained popcorn ceiling talking about their future by wan streetlamp light.

Sound flares in the TV's speakers, this is laughter, something else, words. Words in cadence or by rote or doesn't matter, detached, how the speakers are the making the sound of two people speaking, with all the words seeming incidental. But it's the repeated phrase that makes him realize what he's watching, pay attention—is all time is all the time—a commercial for batteries adapted from a well-known skit out of *Ian Lundy's Paper Caravan*, and how this would have set her off on a rant, using words like defile or desecrate or look how lazy.

You can be dramatic, too, he says, barely aloud, then turns the TV off before the punchline. He begins to haul himself up but stops, sits there a moment. It's bleary what he sees but it's himself and only himself, his chiaroscuro features in the black screen, and he's smiling—the slight tension he feels at the corners of his mouth is a smile. He's imagining what she might have had to say about this and it makes him laugh but only briefly because there is nothing funny going on here. In truth it would have worried her. She would have stared at him with her lips in a straight line, fill in the blank. She would have tried to make light of the situation. She would have said he was turning completely mental, using an accent he would have and would now only be able to identify as British. But she wouldn't have laughed because it would have deeply worried her, what he'd thought he'd seen—his son's face, could've been.

His phone begins to make the sound of someone strumming a guitar, which is his alarm, which means it's 7:00 a.m., and he heads for the kitchen, still in his briefs and tee.

Laminate flooring, plain white walls. She'd wanted parquet flooring but he didn't and after she died he effaced the color from the accent walls throughout the house, rolling white over the geometric patterns she'd painted freehand in vibrant hues of blue and yellow and it was not something he'd done out of spite but just something to do, some easy mindless task to make those first days go by. That was seventeen years ago but still there are times when he can't do something so simple as heat up a cup of coffee without phasing out of reality for a few moments.

Coming up behind her where she stands at the stove amid smoke and music and crackling grease and how the music sounds like this, like sweat and the taste of it on her neck and her low soft moan in the shape of a smile as he places his hand on the boy taking shape inside her, and she's telling him that she so desperately wants coffee she believes it might be worth the risk, ha ha, and how all this is a dull sound somewhere.

A dull chink as he places an enameled cup of day-old coffee in the microwave, 7:06 so says the numbers in garish green, alone, smile fading from his lips. This is how he remembers her, how she exists, not in the choregraphed moments framed for display on the dining room sideboard but lurking in mundane tasks—how memory can conspire with a grief so abiding that it draws out of from even the most ordinary motions a moment from the cherished past all slurred color and sound and mood.

He shuts the microwave door and sets the timer. He watches the cup spin slowly in the sallow drone.

Years ago he'd said to a client, Get rid of them. He was what they used to call a Senior Streamline Advisor and he had liked that job because it sent him places, gave him a good excuse to be away from home, staying in comped hotel rooms where he could do his parenting remotely.

He still works for Telos Consulting but no longer as a fieldman, something else he was once called, and father and husband. Now he holds the title of Interdepartmental Buffer Analyst and largely sits in a cubicle where the hours are perforated by the mundanities of which they're comprised: meeting invites, email pings, the long trilling of his phone. This is all white noise, and so too the memory.

How the client had been staring at him. They were sitting at a large conference table with eighteen empty chairs and the client stared at him and said, Get rid of them?

Fire your team, he'd told the client. Get rid of them.

They were seated perpendicular to each other with the client at the head of the table, a bulky man with dandruff on his shoulders and a ruddy face that began to blink at him. It appeared as if he'd never heard those words in that order before and was still piecing together their meaning. He wore a clip-on tie and regarded a spot on the wall as if for further council, a second opinion.

The client had said, Meaning what?

Meaning they're no good. Or they're mediocre. Whatever you want to call it. The issue is not time management or resource management. In fact, from what I've observed, all of that is being handled quite well. Efficiently, is what you want to hear. Your project managers are doing a great job, the best they can with what they have. And that, unfortunately, is the problem, what you don't want to hear. What you need is not an increase in recruitment efforts, but a reworking of the process itself. You need more stringent standards.

In truth the client had been a boutique ad agency, Patina Media, operating out of Buffalo. The bulky man was just who he'd interfaced with. He waited for the bulky man to respond but all the bulky man did was stare down the length of the table, eyes narrowed, as if trying to see something far away.

It's like this, he'd explained to the bulky man. Say I have a can of red paint. And then I go out and get, say, five more cans of the same red paint. And then I empty the contents of all the cans into a vat. The paint doesn't get any brighter, there's simply more of it.

Before he knows it the workday is over and he's standing in the elevator on his way down to the lobby, staring at his reflection in the door. The door is of brushed steel and his reflection is little more than a dull sheen smeared over the metal, but still there's something in its bearing, its demeanor, grim and humorless and somehow angsty. He is alone in here, a figure in a button-down and pair of chinos with a backpack slung from one shoulder. Think of the kid. Think of the kid walking home alone from the bus stop, his schoolbag decorated with pithy Ian Lundy phrases written in Wite-Out. The elevator hums in the shaft, digital numbers tracking the descent. He steps closer to the door but nothing comes into focus. But, then, maybe. Maybe this is what his son might have come to look like.

The door slides open with a simulated chime not unlike the train's, how time lurches, fidgets, with shapes and colors scrolling past, shapes of homes and trees. It was Queens and then it was Peekskill, in a home with a master bedroom, already making decisions about how they'd raise the child growing inside her. Watching the late sun glint off the Hudson River, he remembers a joke she'd made. Some call it parenting, she'd said. Others call it indoctrination.

On his way home he stops off at the gas station for some more bang-snaps and a tallboy. He's already had one on the train ride back but can go for another. He takes one out from the row of fridges thrumming along the back wall and sets it on the counter. The attendant here knows him by face and calls him My Friend.

"How are you doing, My Friend?"

He doesn't tell him the truth. He removes from a small display rack six, seven, make it ten boxes of whack-pops while a small fan oscillates beside the register, stirring a stink of sweat and coffee grounds.

"You like those lots, My Friend? Pretty Fun, huh, My Friend?"

He nods and smiles but doesn't tell the attendant, whose name is there on a nametag he's never bothered to read, that he used to buy these for his son when his son was just a boy. He doesn't tell him that he and his son used to go out on the driveway in the dusk sometimes to chuck great handfuls of them at the pavement, and how those were about the only times they shared a smile. He doesn't tell the attendant how his son's laugh sounded not only because this would be a strange thing to share, but because he can't. He doesn't remember. Or the sound of his voice. How these memories have become just as estranged, with no sound save the bangs and the snaps and the crackling orange light.

He collects his change and takes the paper bag off the counter and tells the attendant to have a good one. Outside the evening is cool, the last colors failing in the sky and the shadows all gone from here, figures standing at the gas pumps. He's nearly back to his car when he hears something that makes him stop, a hissing sound loud and taut, and he stands there with the paper bag in hand, watching across the lot a woman inflating a bicycle's rear tire at one of the air pumps.

He remembers the first sound his son had ever made. He remembers the sound of the machinery, the frantic beeping and how they pushed him out of the room and carted his wife away down the hall while nurses had to hold him back. He remembers the look on the doctor's face, and he remembers his son's final sound. He remembers the cicadas and the muffled thump in the ceiling and then the steady, lazy drone of the cicadas.

It's his phone that brings him back, vibrating against his thigh, a text message from his father. The limited preview of the message displayed on the screen reads:

Have time . . .

He doesn't bother to read the rest.

Bang:

The father, the man, the father said to the son, "Come here."

The son was sitting on the couch watching cartoons and he looked over at the father but did not move, six years old, feet just touching the floor. The father stood there in the doorway. He had the son's shoes in his hand. Then he didn't. They went tumbling over the floorboards.

"Put them on," he said. "I want to show you something."

He watched the son slip his shoes on and tie them, each in turn, making the loops and knots, realizing he'd never taught him how to do any of that. Then he led him out through the back door and onto the driveway. It was late evening with the sun going down behind the trees, ruddled leaves, smell of chimney smoke drifting on the wind. The son was a gawky kid even for his age, reticent, softspoken, with eyes that never seemed to look but glance. He glanced at the little box the father took out of his jacket pocket.

"You know what these are," the father said. It was a question or it wasn't. It could have been an accusation.

The son stood there. Birds chittered in the trees. The father opened the box and removed the plastic packet that contained little white sacks packed in sawdust. He ripped open the plastic and took out one of the sacks and held it by its twined end. It looked like a small Hershey's Kiss or maybe a small cherry. The boy glanced at it where it hung between the father's fingers and looked away, the faded pavement, dead weeds in the cracks.

"Bang-snaps," the father said. "You've seen these before. Maybe you haven't."

The boy said, "Pop showed me these."

"Right. 'Course he has." He looked at the boy's shoes. "Your pop," he said, "he used to get me these too, sometimes, when I was a kid. Smoke bombs, sparklers, all that stuff. Used to set off these m80s—blockbusters. Neighbors up and down the block would be calling the cops. He show you any blockbusters?"

The son shook his head.

"You wouldn't like those," the man said. "They aren't like these."

He raised his arm and pitched the snap-it at the ground and the boy flinched at the sound it made. The man saw this and wanted to ridicule the boy, the son, and had to stop himself.

He said, "I thought Pop showed you these."

The son didn't answer.

"He had you throw one of them," the father said.

"He threw it."

"And you didn't like it." There was always something there in his voice, a measure of contempt, no matter the topic of words. You could not call it conversation. You could not say they ever talked to each other or had dialogues. They communicated in the most primitive sense. Yes, no, angry, sad. It would later develop that their frequent arguing would be the closest they'd get to conversation.

The boy stood there looking down at the pavement.

Just the other day the boy had asked him for help with his homework, something. The man had told him to speak up, stop mumbling. He never looked at the boy. The question was about life science, insects, why are cicadas so loud or how do they make the sound they make, something like that. He didn't know the answer. Why the hell should he? The kid was always asking questions like that, why do leaves change color or what happened in such and such battle of such and such war, and he wondered how many times did he have to tell the kid. He told him that his wife would have known. He only referred to her as his wife now, denying the boy a mother. But it was a lie. She wouldn't have known the answer either. He only said it so the boy would leave the room and he could go on sitting there, watching a commercial for laundry detergent.

He pinched up another popper out of the sawdust and held it out to the son.

"Go on," he said. "It's fun."

The son took it without looking. He stood holding it in the palm of his hand like something broken.

"Go on," the father said again. "Like this." And the boy flinched again and the father watched him. He told the boy those blockbusters would have made him wet himself.

Then he said, "Just try it. It's different when you're the one doing it."

The son closed his hand around the whipper and raised his fist, brought it down. A prick of orange light flashed against the pavement. He glanced at the father. Then he looked at him, smiled. He held out his hand.

He sits in his cubicle watching words unfurl across the screen while his fingers flit over the keys. Nor do the sounds they make seem attached to the action or the sentences to their meaning. *Deadline, regret,* these words are vague noises in his mind. The office has a drone to it. The email he's typing is about a deliverable that will be late due to some reason he hasn't figured out yet. He sits reading over what he's so far typed, certain words and phrases, *unfortunately, regret to inform, unforeseen complications,* means nothing, the boilerplate excuses. He thinks what else he might type but nothing makes sense, and then he realizes he's been hearing something. He stops, listens.

He listens to a hissing sound, pressurized, coming in spurts so loud and stark that the sound itself seems silhouetted by the office quiet. His head is turned away from his monitor now and he's staring at a picture pinned to the gray tackboard wall of his cubicle but doesn't see it. From behind the wall comes a long oscillating hiss, and it's all he can hear and think and see—that awful time one year ago, slowly ascending the steps to his son's room, calling out his name while cicadas hummed in the afternoon heat.

Now he's standing. He's standing and looking over the tackboard wall into the adjacent cubicle, watching a coworker clean out her keyboard with a can of compressed air, the way she guides the long red straw of the can up and down the rows of keys, ejecting dust and crud and now she stops.

She stops and looks, is looking at him. At first she says nothing. At first she smiles. Then the smile recedes and it's the way her lips move, making shapes that do not seem to match the words, which form an apology or make the sound of one.

He doesn't speak. His jaw feels slack, eyes rimmed red and sunken from another sleepless night of throwing bang-snaps off the deck, of lying in his sweat in the pullout in the wake of a recurring dream.

In this dream he was pushing a mower over the lawn. Last night it was a mower, the night before last it was a snow blower. But his wife, she's always standing in the same spot, doing the same thing: talking to someone in the doorway. He cannot tell who she's talking to or what they're saying. All he can hear is the mower, or the blower. Blowing leaves across the parched lawn. Even last night when in the dream he had turned the mower off all he could hear was the drone of the motor. They were staring at him, or that is how it looked, with their mouths moving, miming out his name, but all he heard was the motor going all the time is all the time.

The office has this drone to it, fluorescents humming their bland light. Her lips shape themselves to the beginning of a word but she says nothing, this coworker, her nervous laugh and smile. There are others nearby but they are not paying attention to them.

He sits finally without a word and finds himself staring at the picture pinned to the tackboard wall. The picture is of his son, after one of his little league games, the yellow jersey, the white pants. He did not take this picture nor can he remember the name of the team. Grass stains, dirt stains, dust. His son is posing in the picture, bat angled over his shoulder, ready to slam one out of the park, he imagines, likes to imagine. It was his own father who'd taken this picture, who'd practically raised the boy. He'd thought maybe things would get better as his son grew, as he developed a personality and had thoughts that weren't expressed through long grating shrieks. But the older he got the more unbearable it became to be around him, the way his face changed, the latent features becoming apparent. He had her high cheek bones and sharp nose and her sense of humor.

There was the time his son was watching a movie in his room, a show, watching something, British voices and a lot of laughter. He could hear it faintly from the home office and he went out into the hall and stood outside the boy's door, listening, hand gripping the knob. He could tell from the exaggerated speech that it was a *Paper Caravan* skit but he didn't know which.

Then he did. He heard the famous line—*is all the time is all the time*—some traveling magician's whacko incantation he'd never understood. But she had loved that skit, loved the actor. She would have loved the quotes scrawled across their son's door, would have taken up a marker herself to add her own favorites. But it had only made him despise the boy even more, how he'd decorated his door with those senseless phrases in some lame attempt to commune with the mother he never knew except from stories, home videos, pictures on the sideboard. Sometimes he caught the boy standing in front of the bathroom mirror, tracing the shape of his nose. In the hallway the father stood there listening, gripping the knob till his knuckles turned white. Then he splintered the wood with his fist and went back into his office while laughter flared behind him.

In his cubicle, his phone begins to ring, a twinkling xylophone riff that strikes up so loudly in the silence it gives him a start. The caller ID says *Dad.* He lets it go to voicemail but his father doesn't leave one. He remembers the text message his father had sent the day before and decides to read it.

Have time to talk? I know someone who'd be happy to help you out.

He means with selling the house. For weeks now his father has been nagging him to sell, to get out of there, move on, enough is enough. She would have told him that he wasn't trying to be difficult but only wanted to help, and he would have said that the only way his father knows how to help is by being difficult, to which she would have said they were just going in circles. She would have said he was being dramatic, sleeping in the basement, washing himself in the outdoor shower, refusing to go to the second floor. She would have told him to listen to his father, he knows what's best. But she didn't know the man his father had become, a widower same as he and no longer a conductor but a recently retired MTA train dispatcher who, with his abundance of free time, could not help himself from attempting to supervise the minutiae of lives that were not his own. Even the real estate agent who had helped him close on his new house upstate had almost dropped him as a client.

His father calls again and he silences the ringtone, leaves his phone there on the desk to mutely flash Dad in bright LED-white while he heads for the bathroom to splash some cold water on his face.

Snap:

The father was in the kitchen fixing himself a drink.

The son was in his room.

They had gotten into an argument and that is where each had ended up. The argument was about a call from one of the son's teachers, or at least that was how it started. Apparently the son had cut his summer chemistry class again. It was chemistry or it was math or history. It was an excuse. The argument was a lot of yelling and banging that devolved at a certain point into cruel and spiteful words that the father found too easy to say, eager to say, how he relished in the hurt look the son struggled to conceal. How the son was a fuckup. How he had been and always would be. How he'd killed his mother on his way out of her. This is what the argument was about—what every argument was ultimately about.

The father stood in the kitchen stirring his drink with his finger. He knew it was not nor had it ever been the boy's fault, though it had taken him a long while to understand this, to admit it. She had always been certain that she wanted children, he had only been certain that he did not want to lose her. Then he lost her anyway, found himself stuck with the thing that had killed the person he loved most in this world. He remembered how the baby had cried all through her funeral, somber speeches punctuated by harsh shrieks. At a certain point during the sister's eulogy, he finally asked a relative to take the baby outside. He didn't call the baby by its name. She had wanted to name the child after her father and that is what he told people when they asked, nothing more.

The father felt ashamed whenever he thought about it now, and all the other things he'd said to his son over the years. On the son's fifth birthday, when the father had believed him old enough to understand, he'd told the son exactly what he'd done to his own mother. It had been a small gathering of close family, grandparents, an uncle and an aunt from his wife's side, and they all sat there in wordless shock. Then he told the boy to blow out the candles. "Go on," he'd said, slightly drunk, the son sobbing at the far side of table while the grandparents tried to console him. "Make a wish."

In the kitchen the father took his finger out of the glass and put it in his mouth, whiskey and ginger ale. Long shadows were sprawled across the room, crumpled in corners.

Upstairs the son was quiet.

He could hear the cicadas throbbing out in the yard, hundreds or thousands or more. A brood had emerged that summer, billions of juvenile cicadas come up from the earth after seventeen long years to finally grow old and die. He thought about the time when the son was three, sitting on the floor in the living room and beating clumsily on a toy bongo set that had been gifted by an aunt while he stood in the kitchen with the phone to his ear, listening to a rep from an adoption agency explain the process. All he remembered now was how the rep had told him, at least fifty times, that putting a child up for adoption was not giving up. He had given up in different ways. The son had become someone he merely tolerated, was obliged to raise. Even when he told the son that he loved him, seldom as that was, he knew the words were perfunctory and the love itself just as superficial and rote. He never knew for certain how his son had learned to swim or ride a bike.

The father held the drink in his fist. He drained it quickly and made another and he was capable of this, of harboring some hatred despite the unfairness of it. His wife would have called him an ass, an idiot. She would have called him a piece of shit and he would have known she was right but it wouldn't have mattered, and this is what frightened him most of all, this fact, or what he believed to be the truth of it—that he would always blame the boy for his wife's death.

He was making a third drink and getting angry all over again when he heard a muffled thump in the ceiling, felt it in his chest, a kind of hollow reverb that rang out in harmony with the ebbing drone of the cicadas.

The next morning, sitting at a red light about twenty minutes away from the train station, his phone buzzes. It's not a text message this time but an email. He doesn't recognize the address save for the domain, hhrealestate, a popular agency based in Westchester County. He already knows what the email will be about but reads it anyway, skims through it.

. . . your father gave me . . . sell . . . interested . . . would love . . . feel free . . .

The light turns green. The car behind him sounds its horn.

Five minutes later he slows the car and pulls off to the side of the road. The road is a quiet backroad flanked by overgrown fields, and he sits awhile staring out the windshield, hands still gripping the wheel.

He cuts the engine. He is sweating slightly. Heat crinkles beneath the hood and there is sunlight is falling through the windows, dust standing on the dash. He takes out his phone and calls his father.

His father picks up on the second ring and before he can even say hello the son tells him to stop, just stop.

"Stop with what?"

"The house. I'm not selling the house."

"Did that real estate agent ever reach out to you?"

"Are you listening to me?"

"I hear you."

"That's not what I asked."

"Are you still going to that group?"

He lowers the phone and presses the top of it against his chin. He can hear his father's voice down there, calling his name.

He says, "Dad, Dad. Listen." He's still holding the phone to his chin, talking over his father's voice. "I am not selling the house," he says, steadily, and again, louder, a third time. The last time he says it, he's screaming the words into the receiver.

There's a silence after that. In the field wildflowers blue and white and yellow heel and shiver in the wind and there is everywhere the electric pulse of insects.

"Dad?" he says. He puts the phone back to his ear. "Dad?" Clouds move past the sun and bands of shadow drift, ripple across the land.

"I'm here." His father's voice is deep and textured, years of smoking and yelling at passengers over the PA. "I'm still here." And the way his father's voice carries a gesture—a hand on his shoulder he can feel the weight of it even as he sits here miles away in the car amid engine clacks and dust motes, and he wonders if he'd ever spoken to his own son in such a way. He remembers opening the door to his son's room. He remembers his son lying there crumpled on the floor, eyes gawking sightlessly at the wall while cicadas throbbed in the heat and a can of compressed air lay overturned on the desk.

He takes a deep breath and says, "I had this dream. Keep having this dream. I'm out front doing yard work, mowing the lawn. One time it's I'm mowing, another I'm blowing leaves, power washing the siding. But Claire is there. She's always there standing in the front door, talking to someone. I can't see who she's talking to. It's just a silhouette, which I don't know how because."

He stops here a moment, wets his lips with the tip of his tongue. His father is silent. There were the times his father had tried to console him, telling him not to blame himself, be too hard on himself. Times when he'd broken down completely and confessed or at least that's what it had felt like, like something that he had to relieve himself of, that would not be true unless he said the actual words—that he failed the boy, failed his son.

"I know it's him," he says. "In the dream. The silhouette, it's tall, you know? Grown. But I know it's Michael. I know it's him but I can't see him. It's the just the shape of him, of maybe him."

He stops again. With his other hand he squeezes the wheel till his knuckles go white. Then he releases.

"I don't know how he looks," he says. "How he might've looked. I think about that sometimes, what he might've looked like as a grown man, as a father himself maybe."

Still his father is quiet. There is just his breath coming through the phone, falling, somehow, warm on his ear.

Four weeks later he watches from the window a red Mercedes coupe pull into his driveway, sunlight gleaming on the hood. The woman behind the wheel sees him, waves, and he steps back to let the curtain fall. He still isn't sure why he's agreed to this.

At the door he greets her, then forgets her name by the time she steps inside. "What a lovely place," she's saying, "how lovely."

He wonders how she's able to make such an assessment by standing in the foyer. Lovely, charming, quaint, gorgeous, she likes these words and others out of the real estate lexicon. In the kitchen he interrupts her description of the room's flow to offer her coffee, water. She declines. She's eager to see the rest of the house. She's a lanky woman in twill pants and blouse who has a peculiar habit of listing aloud the positive features of each room she enters, embellishing even minor details with picturesque descriptions that make him bite the insides of his cheeks, thinking how Claire would have had a field trip with this one.

And it is easier than he thought it would be, moving up the stairs to the second floor. He does not climb or ascend but just moves. The agent comments on the railing, the paneled risers. She calls the home office an audacious space, which he doesn't quite understand, nor does he ask for clarification.

The last room he shows her is his son's.

If she has any thoughts about the words or dent in the door she keeps them to herself. He reaches for the knob but stops, stands there a moment, noticing or re-noticing, reading the words encircling the rose:

Is all the time is all the time.

Written in Wite-out.

"We don't have to go in there," the real estate agent says. "Your father told me. I'm sorry."

He moves his head slightly but doesn't look at her. He opens the door, stands there with his back pressed against the scrawled words, hand gripping the knob. The splintered wood scratches at his shirt as he makes room for her to enter, which she does, hesitantly, almost shyly. But soon she's prattling on about size and floorboards and natural light. There are the words stenciled on the wall, the posters hanging at angles. The bed is unmade. A ripped garbage bag lies wadded on the floor and dirty laundry spills from the closet door. The belt is around his waist.

He realizes the real estate agent is speaking to him. Her voice seems to travel from far away. He looks up from the spot on the floor where he had found his son and stares at her. She's waiting for a response, but he isn't sure what she's said, nor does he ask her to repeat herself. He looks down again. She's wearing things on her feet called shoes, standing in the spot where he'd knelt trying to shake his son awake.

"Anyway," she says, perhaps sensing that he's drifted off from the moment, "it never hurts to make connections. Keep your ear to the ground."

He nods because such a thing as a nod can go here. He reaches into his pocket, mutters something at the time displayed on his phone's screen and makes something up about some work he needs to get done.

"Clients," he says. "You know how it goes."

He does not shut the door to his son's room. They leave, and he shows her to the front, thanking her along the way, apologizing for having wasted her time, to which she assures him he hasn't. As he's opening the front door, she says, "What is it you do? If you don't mind my asking."

"Consulting," he tells her. "Telos." It's a large firm and he feels halfway prideful saying the name aloud.

She stands there on the landing. "Telos," she says. She looks down for a moment and laughs, softly, a private joke. She stares at him through the screen door. "I've worked with your firm before."

"At H and H real estate?" he says.

"No. This was five years ago. Patina."

He stares searchingly over her shoulder, trying to remember. Then it comes to him. He remembers the logo and the conference room with the broad windows and large table and he remembers the bulky man with the ruddy face and what he'd told him to do. He can feel his cheeks going hot.

"The ad agency," he says, but the words are dry and brittle in his mouth. He's expecting her to yell at him, curse him out, berate him.

Instead she tells him she never much liked that job, never cared for it. She thanks him. She tells him that getting fired from that job was the best thing that had ever happened to her, aside from meeting her husband, which she never would have had she still been working for Patina Media.

"Three years ago," she says. "Was showing him an apartment down in Ossining. Now we have a little one on the way, if you can believe it." She places her hand on her stomach. "Just found out a few weeks ago. Crazy," she says, "how things work out in the end."

He stands there staring at her stomach, smiling in a way he knows is creepy, but there's no helping it.

"Well," she says. "You have my info. Let me know if anything changes."

He watches her walk to her car. Before she can start the engine he calls out to her, halfway out the front door and waving his arm for attention.

“Hold on,” he says, and goes back into the house. A minute later he emerges with a few small boxes bundled in his hands.

He walks the flagstone path and proffers them without a word through the open window. She accepts, tentatively. She holds up one of the boxes and reads aloud the words printed on the front. “Bang-snaps,” she says, and looks at him as if for clarification.

He shrugs. He says, “I don’t know. To celebrate.”

She smiles politely. “Take care,” she says, and rolls up the window.

When she’s gone he’s left standing there in the driveway, new weeds in the cracks, listening to the sound that silence makes: birds, wind, leaves, tattered shreds of cigarette paper skidding over the faded pavement. In the distance, the ebbing drone of an engine. That is all. It is early spring, and the cicadas won’t be out for another few months.

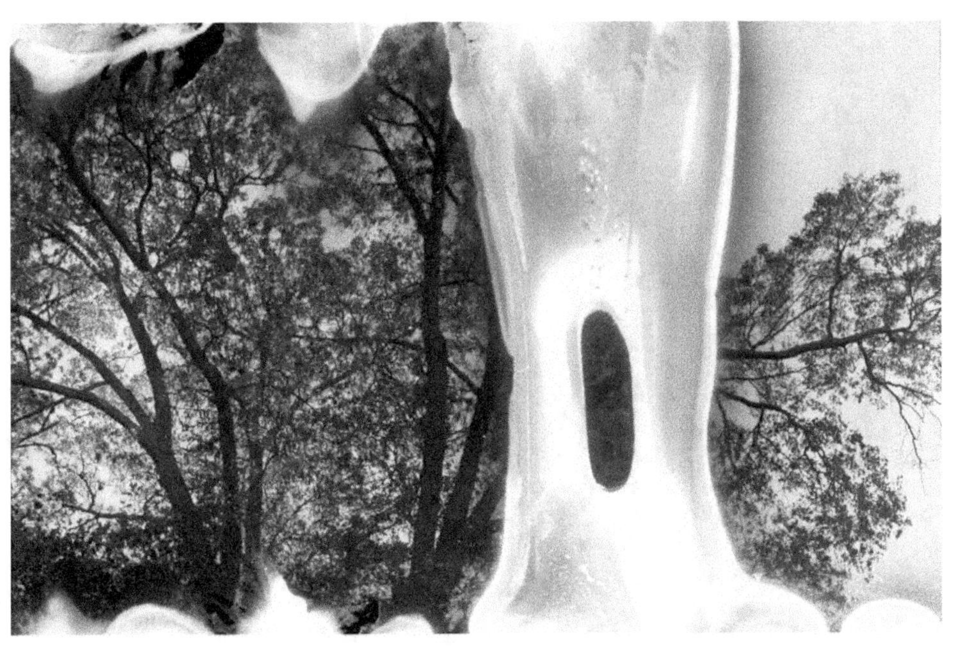

Strange Neighborhood 2

/ Susanna Herrmann

Strange Neighborhood 1

/ Susanna Herrmann

Orpheus, Far from the Abyss

Meagan Daine

Orpheus, I have something to tell you.

Do you remember when we used to climb the dusty hill and push through tangled thorns to reach the eucalyptus grove? The spicy smell of trees. The strips of bark, long as we were tall but fragile, light to hold and crack for the scent to anoint our hands. Slender leaves falling onto thick green grass, the cool grass rising in stalks, mounds, hillocks wild with bell-shaped yellow flowers. Wood sorrel. You taught me to pluck the stems and suck their sour juices. Remember?

Orpheus. Last night I dreamed we were walking up that hill again, and I was happy because I felt you'd forgiven me.

Years have passed since I last heard you sing, Orpheus. But I've only recently begun to mourn you. To let my silences be filled with our unsaid words.

Do you hear them?

Do you remember the place where we met - that house on a hill, where a cool marine breeze streamed through our windows in the mornings and brought with it the peal of distant bells?

We were tenants then, you in one room, I in another. A miracle of possibility. My window faced a garden where a Ficus tree shook its leaves like coins onto a limestone path. Yours opened onto a courtyard where sunlight sank deep gold in the afternoon. Mornings heavy shadows lay there, and so did you, curled under a yellow blanket and dreaming, I imagine, of melodies you'd hummed the night before.

Each morning I stood and let the sheets fall from my body, looked out my window toward the bells and planned the day—things to do, schedules to keep—taking in light and sounds and scents without thought.

Mistakes to fix, tasks to achieve: If I thought of you, it was only in that context.

Then one day I turned from the window and saw an ivory folder on my desk, its surface dotted with petals from a bouquet of baby blue-eyes. I picked up the folder, brushed away the petals, and opened it.

Inside were several sheets of linen paper. The first said colors within and bore your signature. The second was strewn with points, curves, and lines: A composition. A song that you had written for me.

I'm married now, Orpheus. Did you know?

To a man I met when I was in love with you.

I am still in love with you.

After the song, I started watching you. Silent. Hopeful. I thought from now on all your music would be for me, but to my consternation, you went on living as before. You took your fill of life, in fact. Two glasses of wine at a concert. A conversation with professors, waving your French cigarette. An affair with a cellist who performed your work the way it sounded in your heart, despite the fact that she'd never been there.

I didn't understand what all this meant. How you could sing to me once and then stop. So I took on a parallel life, working and studying, filling my days with things to do, tasks to achieve. I met a man who threw great parties, some of which you attended. You and I would stand on opposite sides of a room, hearing music pound like a heart, talking and laughing with the crowd while moving slowly, indiscernibly closer to each other, until we stood back-to-back.

I remember hearing the rhythm of your words like a counterpoint to my mindless chatter. I had a throbbing desire to turn and taste your sweat.

Did you feel it, Orpheus?

You must have. Because when the cellist arrived and stood in the doorway, waiting, I glanced back at you, and our eyes met, and you caught your breath before you went to join her.

We live in an apartment now, Orpheus. My husband and I.

It's carpeted. Quiet. With all-new fixtures.

There are two bedrooms, in one of which we sleep. The second is an office lined with books. Hundreds, maybe thousands of old, misused books with cracked spines and flaking pages. I sit beneath them at a heavy desk to write.

One night soon after we moved in, I dreamed that water started pouring from those books. It filled the office, and I swam until I drowned.

I died in the dream, Orpheus.

I found myself floating in an orb of darkness, which was pricked intermittently by pinpoints of light. They came in pulses, slowly, then faster and brighter. I felt like something magnificent was arriving.

Then, little by little, they dimmed, and finally ceased.

I woke thinking of a poem.

A day came when the cellist had practice, and the man who gave parties was out of town, so for the first time in months, you and I were alone.

We decided to walk into the city. Up windy streets, past stony buildings we'd seen countless times. It was only exercise at first, but then it started to rain. A cold, whipping rain that shocked us alive.

We looked at each other with a startled laugh. You saw a bus stop ahead and ran for it, shouting back at me, hurry, hurry. Sheets of rain and leaves fell all around us. People rushed past, dashing into doorways, ducking into idling cars. You reached the stop and leapt onto the bus. It was packed with bodies. You edged among them and reached back for me. I took your hand. You pulled, I held on, but I couldn't fit on the bus. There was only room for a single foot. For a moment I stood dangling, suspended by an arm, as rain poured over me and the engine rumbled. Our hands were wet. Hard as you held me, they slipped, and I fell back onto the sidewalk.

The doors shut.

The bus motored away.

I stared after it in dumb confusion.

Now what? Should I run after it? Take cover and wait?

I didn't know what you'd do. If you'd come back for me. I didn't know where I was. I felt the rain turning to ice as it slid down my neck. My throat tightened with irrational fear that I'd done something irreparably stupid.

Then a hand grasped my arm.

I looked up and saw you, somehow, standing next to me, droplets clinging to the lashes of your laughing eyes.

Relief surged into my chest. I felt ...

Whole.

You slipped out of your gray wool coat and held it over us.

Time passes without consent.

I'm not ready to grow old.

I still want

That night you came into my room.

I'd left the door unlocked, thinking maybe ...

And you did, and I sat in breathless anticipation as you stood adjusting to the darkness. I watched you until you could see, Orpheus. And I sensed there was something wrong. Your black hair was wild around your head. Your eyes, always warm and brown, were feverishly bright.

After a moment you came to my bed and knelt to see if I was awake. I smiled. So did you, but your smile was fragile, desperate. In a hollow whisper, you said she knows.

I wasn't sure what you meant. I knew she was the cellist. I felt a surge of joy that I was in your heart. But there was more, there had to be more, some reason her knowing had brought you to the brink of a precipice.

I waited. Breathing in your scent of musk and cigarettes and sweat. Feeling your heat on the mattress, your hand near my thigh. My chest rose and fell. Rose and fell. Too many times before a realization finally dawned: You were expecting my response.

I didn't know what to say.

I was a disciple of things to do and tasks to achieve. I thought all answers had to be correct. But when I searched for correctness in this moment, I found none. Panic rose in my throat, desire mixed with the fear of failing to give you what you wanted. I scrabbled to hold onto something that was wisping away. I had no answers. Only the paltriest of questions, which at last was what I offered you: What are you going to do?

You drew back. Smiled again, this time as though you wanted to cry. You took my hand, raised it to your lips, and kissed it. Then you stood up and walked away.

Barberry. Helianthella. Bitter dogbane.

These are the flowers that bloom where I live now.

Sometimes I gather a few in a vase and place them on my desk, where I leave them until the petals crumble into dust.

My husband does not understand why I do this.

He wonders idly at my ability to remember each flower's name. I don't answer because I can't explain what I'm writing to tell you, Orpheus – what I now know, after years of sitting in the shadows of these books, recalling that night when you came to me, anguished in the dark – years of seeking the litany of syllables I should've said, what would've made you stay – that a word, like a note, is a unit of life.

You knew that.

You gave me your life in a song, and when you waited for mine in return, I wavered. I feared I would give you the wrong life, one that was flawed or unfinished or worst of all unworthy, so in the end, I gave you nothing.

I'm sorry.

I'm sorry.

This is what I have to say.

I will never speak these words, Orpheus.

You're too far from me now to hear them.

But I write because their power—unread, unspoken, unknown even by the man who took your place in my life—I am, at last, beginning to perceive.

Hartsong

Erin Birdsall

Mam is doing it again: waiting at the kitchen window above the leaky tap, staring down the side of the mountain to the line where the bog kisses the first slender birches of Tully's Wood. She is listening for something I can't hear, untouchable as her own dead mam's crystal.

The chipped blue mug in my hand clinks as I set it down on the counter, and her head jerks. "You're using your sister's mug," she says.

"All the other ones are dirty."

"But it's hers."

"I was making some tea. Don't make a fuss."

"That's your sister's mug, so. Katie's coming home tonight. I can feel it. No reason to treat her things like Father Aloysius already said the words at her grave."

Back it goes, sitting in a circle of dust.

"You've never been much for sense. Even at eighteen years of age. Not a feather of sense in that great odd head," she mutters, and turns toward the window.

With Mam, there are three things I can't do.

The first is use the blue mug.

The second is talk about my Da. When I do that, she pulls at her hair and presses her thumbs into her bottom teeth and doesn't talk to me for days. Once in a while she'll be so upset that she'll forget to go to town to do the shopping, so when I was younger, sometimes the only thing left were the beers in the fridge. That second rule wasn't hard to follow, when breaking it meant I'd starve.

And the third thing I only tried once ten years ago, when I was eight and Katie was ten. Mam chased us round the house and beat us raw with a copy of *Finnegan's Wake* when she caught us. To this day I don't like reading anything longer than two hundred pages. Trying to follow my runaway sister into the wood wasn't worth the bruises.

They never stopped Katie though. That was only the first time my sister disappeared—over the years she'd wander back and forth from home. She got in a fair bit of trouble with Mam and the local guards for being in and out of school, at least the first few times—before the whole town labeled her a lost cause, before Mam "went away with the fairies" and started having those strange dreams of hers. At first, I hadn't minded Katie leaving. I thought Mam would eventually let me drink out of whatever mug I chose. But no, that's Katie's mug. She'll be home soon. Mam got quiet when Katie was gone. Everything was quiet, then.

I open the cupboard, find a different mug, grab some milk and two bags of Barry's, and put the kettle on. I make two cups, one for me, one for Mam. Out the window, a deer leaps across the bog. We watch as it disappears into shadow.

I am seven. Da says that's the age of wisdom, whatever that means. I am on my Da's knee and his white whiskers scratch my face. He is showing me the picture of the brave warrior Oisín on a snowy horse with Queen Niamh standing beside him with all her pretty golden hair. I wish I had her golden hair instead of plain old brown. I love the Good People. They are all so beautiful and magical and the forests are so thick and green and alive. My Da's voice swells up like the sea, like all the Atlantic is inside his belly.

But then! Oh, my darling! The girth around Embarr's great white breast snapped! he says. And he snaps his fingers right then and his dark eyes pop open wide. I squeal, What happened next?! What happened to Oisín?!

And Da says, I'll tell you! The magic girth fell clear off Embarr, and poor Oisín fell to the ground of the motherland, where all his three hundred years caught up to him in one moment, and he withered up and died right then and there!

My Da crams his eyes tight, crumples onto the rug, making a great boom as he goes, and shivers up into the tiniest ball he can, which isn't very tiny because of his great belly. I jump onto him and he grunts and chuckles and winks at me. You're getting too big, my Norrie, he says, as he takes me in his arms and carries me to my bed.

I ask him if I can be one of the Good People, too? Like Niamh?

Runs in your blood, my girl! On your mother's side, of course, that's where you get all your oddity from, your mam. Don't tell her I said it, though, or she'll beat me, he says, teasing.

I heard that says Mam, laughing and walking into the room with Katie. She's in a good mood. Mam lays Katie down and kisses us both goodnight. I wait until Mam leaves, and then I pull on Da's face, burying my head in his scratchy cheek. His breath smells a little funny—sour.

And I ask him, are those stories real?

He thinks for a moment and says that in the Kingdom they are. Real as God.

Good, I say. I want them to be real. He kisses my head, turns off the light and closes the door. I turn onto my side toward Katie's bed and the window that looks out upon the field in the back of the house. My sheets are soft. I can hear Mam and Da talking soft downstairs, something about the hunt tomorrow morning. This time of year Da wakes up early to go bird-hunting in the wood. Mostly he gets pheasant or duck, sometimes a goose. But he sells the meat to the butcher. Mam likes the extra money, says it means we get something nicer for Christmas. I wish it were Christmas already. I pull my duvet up to my chin and look past Katie, out the window.

The dark of Tully's Wood and the field and the sky are all the same dark, but the mist glitters, glitters like Tír na nÓg, and for a minute Niamh is in that mist and somehow I am Niamh too and we're all made up of the same thing, the same magic. And then a shadow slips across the fog, like one of those silvery little minnows in the river, and my sister becomes very still. Though I can't see her eyes, I know they are watching the shadow run as closely as mine. Normally I'm asleep by now, but Katie likes to stay up late. She's always been that way, up and about at strange hours. Maybe it's because she was born at midnight—they say those people can see the Fair Folk clear as day even when they're in disguise. Katie's pale hair shines, falling like water off her thin shoulders. She rolls over to face me, eyes glinting, and says to me, Nora. We forgot to pray.

I grab a beer out of the fridge. Mam is still staring out the window. Her hands are shaking—they always do unless she's drinking. I take hold of one of them and she doesn't tug away. Remember what you've learned, Nora: if you push too hard, too fast, she'll shatter. Be quiet. Let her come to you. Mam's muttering now, a kettle over heat. I can't make out what she's saying, but I do catch one thing: *—dreams—*

"Dreams, Mam?"

She starts like she didn't know I was there, even though I've been holding her hand a while now. "Strange dreams I've had," she murmurs. "Lots of animals. Gave me a fright."

"What kind of animals?"

"Slippery slidey fish. Ravens, pecking. Those foxes. Red and black and white, witch familiars. And deer, always deer, antlers out to here, out to here ... Matthew, he ...."

"So Da was there?" I ask, testing my luck.

"No ... yes. I don't ...." she says, her voice petering out. Her eyes cloud over, harden.

"Was this like the other dreams you used to have?" I ask.

"No. In this one, he was alive."

She pulls away and starts down the hall. I follow her. "Mam," I say, gently as I can, "You can talk to me. Please."

"I can't," she whimpers, pressing her fingers into her mouth and shaking her head. "I can't!" I put my hand on her arm to comfort her—a mistake.

She wrenches her arm away and pushes past me so hard that I hit the wall, beer sloshing out of the bottle and spilling all over my top. I stand there, dripping. My face is hot, tight.

I can tell that Mam knows what she's done by the way her spine caves in as she faces me. At least she knows that I'm there, that I'm real. She won't look at me. "You're the same, you and him," she says flatly, gazing instead at the beer stains on my shirt. "Living in a fairy world. Always making up stories to make everything sound better than it is. You're liars. Both of you. And ... and ... you both left me here," she moans like a wounded animal, moving toward the staircase. I wipe my hand across my cheek and my mascara comes with it.

"I don't know what you're talking about. Katie was the only one leaving you. Da, well, it wasn't his fault. And I never left you, not once," I say, voice cracking. As she stands in the stairwell, she raises her eyes to meet mine. There's a trace of something there, behind the empty blue—what, anger? Pity? I can't tell.

"God ... I loved him. I did, I swear it," she croaks.

I don't know what to say to her, so all I can do is down what's left in the bottle and wonder whether Katie—or I—will ever be home again.

Me and Katie and Mam and old Auntie Maeve and Auntie Margaret and Cousin Terry have seats in the front row pew. It almost feels like those times when we take the drive to Killarney and my Da reads his poems out loud at the pubs and we sit up front. All the same people are here—the old barkeep who tells good stories, the quiet women who sip at their drinks and gossip in the back, the fat men who watch football and scream at the telly. Auntie Margaret says they're scuttered and people in that state shouldn't be in a church for Godsake. I wish we were in the pub. When my Da reads out loud there, Mam always buys me chips and I suck the salt from under my fingernails. Mam once said that us eating chips together and watching Da reading his poems at the pubs under those dusty lights was her kind of church. I want chips right now but they don't serve chips in real church so I ask Auntie Margaret if we can go get chips after this and she says *Fwisht.* Now stop swinging your feet all around like a hooligan and be a big girl, pet.

Mam doesn't say anything at all. She holds Katie's hand and stares ahead. Her eyes are red and swollen. Cousin Terry hands her a hanky. Terry is almost seven years older than me and two times as loud. He leans over to me and his breath smells like mints and stale smoke. He whispers Oi, Nora. Old Auntie Maeve's arse is about the size of California, don't you think? He smiles and it's funny and I know I should laugh because he's trying to make me laugh but I can't somehow. I don't want to be here, and I don't understand why I have to wear my black frock. We normally don't sit so close to the front—Mam's never liked it here so she likes to sit in the back where no one will notice if she leaves in the middle of Holy Communion. I wish I could spit the wafer out—tastes like paper. Right now I really want chips, more than anything. Salty salty chips. Aunt Margaret gives Terrence the evil eye 'cause he's still leaning and he sits real straight again.

Now Father Aloysius is up at the altar and everyone gets quiet. Katie likes to listen to Father Aloysius. He's very nice in an old way, especially when he came to visit us at home last week. Once he visited school and everyone got to go into the assembly hall and listen to him talk about the Sacred Heart of Jesus and how the church and our school were named after it. There was a picture of Jesus and his heart was glowing and he looked very loving and sorta like my Da but skinnier. Katie sat still as always and I remember Sister Agatha said in front of the class that Katie was the best listener she ever saw. She rang home to tell Mam so, and Mam took us out to the pub that night and got us all chips.

Then Father Aloysius starts to talk about my Da and how he loved God and he loved all glorious green creation and he was a true man of Ireland. And then he starts to say something about how the Lord is mysterious, that it was a shame Matthew Malone had to go as he did, especially with his poor Mary and Katie and Nora left behind. He was a true poet, and we will miss him dearly, but now he is in Heaven, the poor downcast soul, and he has no need for sadness or pain any longer. I liked that part. And then he opens the golden book at the front near the coffin and reads a Psalm out loud that's about hearts and downcast souls and brooks and tears and panting. How could a heart pant? Is that the same as when it beats? Father Aloysius is not explaining anything and now my eyes and hands fidget because I want to know what he's talking about, so I ask Terrence and he says, No idea, he's just telling a story.

And now all I can think of is my Da telling me stories about Oisín and Niamh and reading his poems out loud and the salty chips from the pub that make me so thirsty. My mouth is watering. But this isn't a pub, it's church and they don't have chips. Mam's eyes are tight and staring at her knees as she holds Katie's hand. She's not listening to Father Aloysius.

But Katie is, and even though her cheeks are wet, she is smiling. And now she's giggling, actually, and loudly, too, so people can hear. She is making a holy show of herself. Old Auntie Maeve crosses herself and Auntie Margaret and Terrence's jaws drop. Father Aloysius stops and stares, but not in a mean way. He looks tired. My cheeks are hot and I slide down a little in my seat. For the first time, I wonder whether Katie is mad. Only mad people laugh out loud at their own father's funeral.

Katie had always been odd. Brilliant, but odd. For example, in her third year, Katie asked Sister Estelle if she could play the cello for the annual Sacred Heart Christmas Charity Night. My heart dropped into my bowels. Charity Night was the biggest event of the school year. There was a performance and an auction and all the money raised went to charity, that year to child cancer patients. I'd wanted Charity Night to be my thing ever since my art teacher, Sister Catherine, had asked me to use my "artistic gifts" to create some paintings to sell at the auction. Which was the first time I'd ever been noticed, for anything, ever, mind you. Katie didn't need Charity Night—I did.

Sister Estelle, who was ever the diplomat but who might have been confused, as per usual, as to who she was speaking to, said yes, pet, why don't you come to auditions in two weeks, Monday, after school in the sanctuary, and I'll decide then. Right then I crossed myself and prayed to God, our Holy Mother, and Saint Cecilia that she was terrible.

But I felt guilty for it. In the confessional the next week, I told Father Aloysius about my sin of covetousness and he told me that coveting was dangerous and look what happened to Cain. But he said the Lord has forgiven thee, and now for your penance, my child, say three Hail Marys. So I did that, and I guess the Hail Marys did their job because instead of covetous, now I felt confused, because I realized something—Katie didn't play cello. At least, not that I'd seen. I don't know why it took so long to occur to me that I'd never heard her play the thing, not once. Unless she practiced at a friend's house? But no, Katie didn't have any friends. Had Mam secretly paid for lessons? But no, a family like ours couldn't have afforded it. How, where, when did Katie play? I'd heard her humming something around the house, but she was always quiet, and even when I could hear it, the tune was unrecognizable. And that's when it hit me: Katie was about to make an absolute eejit of herself. And though Charity Night might be all mine at the end of it, she'd take me down with her.

By that fateful Monday, word had gotten around school, so much so that at auditions, I knew that at least half of the so-called Charity Night auditionees in the pews fully intended to leave once they'd watched Katie make a fool of herself. I'd tried to make an excuse not to be there, but as Mam never picked us up until six anyway, it was a lost cause. So instead I huddled in the back pew, smudging the pencil in my sketchbook with my sweaty nose, pretending none of it was happening.

Still, that afternoon I heard Sister Estelle call Katie's name, watched her wander up to the red-carpeted chancel to the great cello shining under the blazing sanctuary lights. What will you be playing for us, Sister asked. Oh it's something I've written myself, Katie said. Her answer reverberated down the aisles, which went dead silent. Except that, two pews ahead of me, Sinead Dunn and Charlie Navan giggled, whispered to themselves. Ignoring them—or oblivious?—Katie picked up her bow like it was a magic wand and she was casting some sort of fairy spell and then I knew it was over for me and Charity Night.

The sound that poured forth—it was alive, heavenly, both strange and familiar. It made the hair on the back of my neck stand up. It was as if the cello knew that the whole world was terrible and wonderful at the same time and only Katie would ever be able to understand it enough to conjure its music. Her song came out of nowhere.

But at least I was still better than her at art. Katie couldn't draw to save her life, though of course Mam put up her stuff around the house. Art was the one class Katie failed in school, and publicly, too. Apparently the assignment was to draw something from life, but when Sister Catherine saw Katie's drawing, she chided her in front of everyone that it clearly didn't follow the assignment. And then for some reason my sister took the paper from the nun's hand, ripped it in half, and threw the pieces at her, then ran out crying. I don't know what exactly she drew but Jenny Grady said it was some sort of giant angel with antlers.

After the art class incident everyone talked about Katie. Their eyes darted back and forth and they got quiet when she walked down the hall, her white-blond hair swishing back and forth. A mad genius, they said. They said she was hysterical, but she never looked it. She always smiled, always laughed, was always so polite to the Sisters, who loved her, except Sister Catherine. She listened. She never did anyone harm, at least not on purpose. Never let any of the rumors touch her. And it was funny, because when she ran off all those times, it was almost like she was more "there" than when she actually was, because for weeks afterward the only name Mam and I'd hear was hers. Poor, mad Katie, born at midnight, run off again into the wood.

I hated her, especially when she left.

But I hated them more for talking about her.

Mam was right: Katie comes bursting in the door right before dinner time. It's the first time I've seen her in weeks. Her longest absence yet.

"Mammy," Katie says, and hugs her—in the embrace, Mam's brittle face softens and her shoulders unwind. And then to me—she grabs my hand and whispers, "I've missed you." Before I can stop myself my mouth wobbles and I smile all the same and say, "I've missed you too."

We set the table together. I do the plates, Mam sets out the silverware (plates break too easily if she drops them), and Katie arranges the glasses for beer and the mugs for when we have tea after. Mam watches out of the corner of her eye as Katie sets down each mug in its place. Purple for Mam, green for me, and blue with the chip in the corner, of course, for herself. Mam smiles, sets the fork and spoon down with careful precision, begins to sing something familiar I can't remember. She has a nice voice when she's lucid, though she gets all bothered when you tell her so. This is her at her best nowadays, singing in the kitchen, happy at the sight of the three mugs on the table in their right spots ... well, three out of four, anyway. Mam bustles over to the stove, stirs something. Thankfully her cooking skills haven't left us quite yet—she always shows off when Katie comes home.

"Are you hungry, Katie dear? I've made a lovely curry, your favorite," Mam says.

"Yes! I could tell as soon as I walked in. All my favorite spices. Smells grand."

Mam smiles. She's a new woman.

It's these times I barely know what to make of her—she's unrecognizable to me. She even bows her head and closes her eyes when Katie prays over the meal. After the Amen she and Katie chitter away about nothing at all—some movie Katie had seen lately? Mam's juiciest tidbits of gossip from Auntie Maeve's latest weekly visit? I try to listen but lose track. It's always baffled me. How do they talk so much about nothing at all, and so little about ... everything? Da and I were alike in that way, shite at small talk, far more at ease telling stories than asking questions—

"Nora," Mam hisses.

"Em, sorry?"

"Katie asked you a question. Pay attention."

"I asked, how's school going?" Katie says, blowing on the bite she's about to take.

"Oh, grand, yeah," I say. Since when has she cared how school was going for me?

"That's it?" Mam looks at me hard. Funny how she never has a problem with my brief answers unless her beloved eldest is home.

"I mean, I don't know, it's alright. Classes are fine. I'm getting by," I say, breezily as I can. "Can one of you pass the chips over here, please?"

"Oh come on, tell me more! I know I've been out two years now but I need you to keep me updated! How are your friends?"

"Haven't seen any of them around lately, have we?" Mam adds lightly, sipping at her already-near-empty pint. She's in fair form tonight. I ignore her.

"Well, what have they been up to?" Katie says.

"Talking about you. Amal and Sinead and Charlie, David and Emma, all of them."

It gets deadly quiet for about half a second. We're all sitting there, chewing in the silence. Then Katie laughs, "How pathetic," but she stops when she sees my face.

"Yeah. Well. Leaving Cert's coming up in June, anyway, and then they'll be gone. So. It doesn't matter. Pass the chips, please?"

But Katie can't take a hint. "Leaving Cert. That's right. Have you decided where you're going to school? Where have you applied?"

Christ, not this. Mam turns toward me, lazy and sharpish all at once. By her look I can tell she slipped a little something extra into her beer glass when I wasn't looking. Soon she'll start slurring her words. I try to find the words before Mam has a chance to speak, but she beats me to it.

"Pet," Mam, says to Katie, gripping my shoulders and shaking me a little, like I'm a doll she's showing off to her real daughter. "This is where you need to talk some sense into your sister. The Natch ... National College of Art and Design is a fine instish ... inshitution. They don't take just anyone—"

"Mam," Katie says, eyes wide. She looks at me and I know she knows she's made a mistake. I focus on the wall behind her head, settle in.

"What?" Mam says, waving her hands about. Her tremor is gone. "She's fine! She's grand. Grand, I mean! I'm only ... it's not like she's M-Michelangelo, that's all. It's not a bad thing! I just don't know what they'll want with cartoons? Or what a decent employer will want with them, is all. That's all. That's all. Jesus, what would a wan like you do in a place like Dublin anyhow? Likely make a right tit of yourself. But anyway, anyway, doesn't matter, they won't take you—"

"Mam!" Katie yells. She's pale. "That's enough."

Mam blinks, saying nothing. Her chair screeches as she gets up, pours herself another glass. She totters to the parlor and turns on the telly, where she'll sulk for the rest of the night.

Meanwhile, Katie and I start doing the dishes in silence. I wash, she dries, and out the window the light slips beneath the woods in the valley, from golden to dusty blue. "I'm sorry," she says, after a while. "I didn't know she'd go after you like that—"

"It's fine."

"You know she didn't mean it—"

"She did. But it doesn't matter, anyway." I lower my voice to a whisper. A smile creeps up onto my face, though it feels wrong there. "I already got in."

"Brilliant," Katie's smile lights up her face. "I always knew you'd get in wherever you wanted to go. Your art is class. Always has been. Why haven't you told Mam?"

I stare at her as we switch washing and drying duty.

"You're joking me. You heard her, didn't you?"

Katie frowns and catches my eye. "Don't listen to her. She's not right, in the head I mean. Touched," she murmurs. I laugh, and Katie's eyebrows furrow. "What? Am I wrong?"

"No. I don't know, it's ... that's what they said about you at school, when you left. 'Touched.' Just sounds funny, coming from you."

"Right. Well, like you said, you'll be gone to Dublin soon enough, won't you? You'll make new friends. Hopefully ones who don't gossip so much," she says, rolling her eyes.

Plates clatter, slipping heavy in my fingers as I set them in the drying rack, harder than I mean to. I grit my teeth. "I said I got in. I didn't say I was going."

"Of course you're going."

"How can I? You said it yourself! Christ, look at the state of her. Unlike some of us, I can't run off so easily, now, can I?"

Katie's pale cheek flushes slightly. Good.

"You think it's easy for me?" she says. She brushes gentle, soapy circles on a plastic plate like it's bone china, staring hard at her hands, past them. "Maybe you don't remember much. But I do. I remember what Mam was like before, back when she laughed and talked and told jokes. Before both of them started drinking so much and then Da died and fucked everything up," she says, articulating the F in 'fucked' like it's a gunshot, a wound I can feel.

"That's our own father you're talking about—"

"He was a good man, Norrie, don't get me wrong. I just ... after he was gone, things changed." Katie looks over through the kitchen to the parlor, where Mam's watching the telly. "I just couldn't stay. She ... broke," she whispers.

As if I didn't know, as if I didn't have to pick up her pieces every single day. "Yes. Well, that's grand for you," I say. Katie's mouth opens, but nothing comes out and she turns back to the sink. The back of my throat feels dry, like there's not enough air in here, so I go to the fridge and grab a beer, and in the silence between us, broken only by the sound of the running tap and my sister's scrubbing, I drain the bottle to the last drop. And then I pour a whiskey. And I down that too. And then another.

"Katie. Tell me. Why do you go to the woods? What are you doing in there?"

"Why do you need to know?

"I'm worried, aren't I? You keep leaving more and more, for longer and longer, and—"

"Well I can't tell you. I'm sorry."

"Why can't you tell me? You don't trust me?"

"It's not time yet."

I don't know what to say to that. I open the window and, together, we look out at the wood for a while, the fog that hides the trees, the trees that hide one another, the black night that hides everything. Katie is silent, and her mouth works, deciding. She pulls me close, whispers. "Look. Someday soon, I'll show you, maybe. Once I know, once I'm sure. I just ... I need time. But that's all I can say." Her eyes flicker toward the dark sky outside and stare past it, as if they can see whole galaxies beyond. Touched, indeed.

The deer were there long before we ever were. They came and went, and came and went, like ghosts in the bog. Da always said there was something about them more human than he expected, so he didn't like to hunt them. One of them, a big stag, he looked at me like he could read the very words on my heart, Mary, he'd told Mam one afternoon that autumn when we were watching telly, I couldn't shoot the beast. And Mam said, You eejit, they're just deer. And he said, God above, I couldn't shoot it. It was white! Mam laughed at that. You're drunk! she said. And then Da started yelling, I'm not, I'm not lying, it was ... like an angel! It, it was divine intervention, me leaving it where it stood! Mam snorted. Really, Matthew. Don't be daft, spouting that nonsense around the girls. Nora's only seven, for Godsake. They hear enough fairy tales from you and Father Aloysius combined. Jesus Christ. Put down your drink, she said, rolling her eyes. Da shook his head and covered his face with his hands.

Then Katie piped up about how she was reading her Bible and there was some love song in there about a lady and a deer was there too and Mam said, Katie pet that's ridiculous, now *fwisht,* I'm watching the telly. I giggled because finally know-it-all Katie got in trouble with Mam. Katie pouted.

But Mam was never one for letting a matter lie. She yelled at my Da again later that night and told him to get back out there tomorrow and stop arguing like he always did and find that buck and bring it home with its insides out. So the next night he took his gun and a six-pack of Fosters and into the woods my Da went.

He came out in a body bag.

"You shouldn't have to be the one to take care of Mam," she says from the doorway.

I am lying on my bed in the dark of our shared bedroom, letting the cool, April night air wash over me from the open window. The irony of Katie telling me this, of all people, staggers me into silence. I don't bother to respond. Instead I look out to the bog on the mountainside, the trees beyond, the lake, the bright moon and twinkling sky above it all—like a painting. The same square of earth I've been staring at through glass since before I can remember.

Katie enters, sits cross-legged on her bed, looking at me, backlit silver.

"What about Auntie Maeve? She could help while you're away. Loves being the martyr, that one."

"Oh, and are you going to be the one to ask her?" I snarl. "Because I won't. But be sure to invite me along when you do, because Lord knows I'd love to watch that play out, knowing how highly she thinks of you, her mad woods-pissing truant niece."

Katie stares at me in shock, and then we both dissolve into weak laughter. It feels good to laugh. We lie there, listening to crickets chirping, wind hushing over the heather. I can feel the silence reach its edge, cresting, a wave on a cliff.

"Nora." Katie turns to me again, and all at once I'm brought back to goodnight kisses, forgotten prayers. "All I'm trying to say is ... it's not your fault, how Mam is," she says gently. "Or your responsibility. You have to know that. We needed her. But she chose to drink—"

"It's not that simple," I say, voice catching in my throat. I have a mild headache. The whiskey is catching up to me.

"Of course it's not. I know that," she says, after a moment. Her voice sounds heavy, tired. "But what is simple is that you're not the one who can fix her. I hope you know you deserve more. Art school, at the very least." She shifts and the duvet rustles. "I ... I may have poked around and found your drawings earlier."

"Illustrations."

"Illustrations, then. They were beautiful."

"Thank you."

"They're of Da's old stories, right?" The wind stills, exhales.

"Oisín and Niamh," I whisper. "Diarmuid and Gráinne. The children of Lír."

Katie nods, looking up at the ceiling. "And Fionn mac Cumhaill, and Sadhbh."

"I don't remember that one. What's it about?"

"It's a good one," she says. "I'll tell you."

And then, there in the dark, the warp and weft of Katie's voice spins tales of the great hunter and dark druids, hazel wands and great loves, deer women, lost children. I remember Da, and fall asleep already in a dream.

We buried him in the Sacred Heart churchyard, like good Catholics ought. He would have thought it proper. But Mam had other ideas. One early morning a few days after the funeral, she ushered us down the side of the mountain to the edge of the woods, where an old stone lay next to a patch of gorse. Katie and I watched as she pulled a hammer and a chisel out of her bag and began carving into the face of the rock. We must have sat there for hours, watching her as bits of stone chipped away, as dust caked in the sweat on her forearms. I remember the cold, wet air seeping up the ends of my fingers and toes, the gnawing in my empty stomach as the shadows of the trees changed from rust to muddy blue to violet. Katie and I stayed quiet, holding hands. It was nightfall when she finally backed away from it, finally spoke to us. His body might be buried in the churchyard, but his spirit won't rest anywhere save here, she said. Read it, she said. And we did. *Matthew Malone, Man of God, Poet, Dearly Beloved. 1956-1999.* It was an unremarkable, moss-covered stone not nearly big enough for the soul of the man lying under it.

"Nora ... Nor."

"Hm, hm." I roll over in my bed to face Katie. The clock displays an unholy hour.

"Mam's whimpering in her sleep. Can't you hear?"

Through the wall behind me, I can hear soft, unintelligible whines, murmurs.

"Fine, fine. I'll go."

My head aches from drinking. I step into her room. Mam is thrashing around, her sheets twisted around her legs like poison ivy vines. Moving over to her bedside, I whisper, "Mam. Mam. It's only a dream." But she is still tossing, her neck taut and her body quivering, moaning like a banshee. I touch her shoulder. "Mam. It's me. I'm here." I switch on the light from her bedside table. Too bright. She sits straight up. I grab hold of her hand as she heaves in and out. "Want to tell me about it?" I say, a little louder. I need her to wake up.

"In the wood," she says, low and prophetical, eyes still shut. She rarely speaks in complete sentences in these moments. Her thumbs press against her teeth. "A ghost—she looks just like him."

"It's okay, Mam. I'm here. There's no ghost."

"He's bound to come for her, out of those woods. Tied in a knot, tied in knot they are, don't go ... don't let her go, Katie, my love."

My heart skitters. "Mam. It's me."

She opens her eyes, which meet mine. "Katie. I want Katie."

I stand there, frozen for a moment. "I know, Mam," I say, and with that I leave her, shutting the door.

When I cross the hall back to our room, Katie's duvet is wrinkled and flat. Her pillow still has a dent from her head. She's gone.

I grab my coat and sprint downstairs.

Mam can't chase you with James Joyce now, Nora.

The dishes are dripping in the rack near the sink. After a split second, I grab the blue mug and smash it to the ground, pieces skittering over the ground like insects over a forest floor.

I step outside, and I run.

The air outside is wet and cool. I can smell the heather and the green as my feet squelch clumsily downhill. It's hard to be quiet on earth like this. The silver mist glows, and I remember Niamh and her golden hair and poor Oisín who fell to the ground and aged three hundred years in an instant. My hair glitters with dew, and for a few minutes I am Niamh again for the first time in ten long years. One of the Fair Folk, running through the mist.

At the edge of the wood, I stop for a second to breathe, to catch my bearings. I feel a bit sick, but that's not important now. The house is far, far up the mountain from here. Here are the first silver birches, glowing under the moon, a patch of gorse, a large stone. I'm at my father's grave—the grave with nobody buried under it. It's smaller than I remember it. I haven't been back in so long. I run my hand along the etched surface of the stone, slick with moss and lichen, darkened with time. The trees rustle.

And then, faintly—a song. I remember it, even all these years later. Even through the trees and the thick of night, it's like the song can see me, guide me. I wind my way through the thin copse of birches and pines into the more ancient thickets, the twisting, outstretched arms of oak and yew, listening.

The dark of the forest envelops me, consumes my figure so that it is merely a shadow among other larger, straighter, older shadows. It's otherworldly here. Tree roots weave through the earth, the coils of sea serpents. Holly bushes prickle my skin as I swipe past them. I can hear the skitterings of creatures in the understory, feel the damp of the forest floor seeping into my shoes as I walk in a half-mile, and another. Though I don't know how long it's been since I started walking—ten minutes? Twenty-five?—I can still hear the music. Everything is still, wild, silent. I follow the song, the song that beckoned Katie, and now beckons me, and probably, in some way, all of us. Closer, and closer. It feels ... golden, a golden thread ....

I'm down on the ground. I've stumbled, tripped over a branch. I regret the beer and the whiskey. I swear to Jesus I'll never drink again. My palms and knees sting from scratches. I want to cry out, but I catch it in my throat, because Katie can't know I followed her. And that is her, up ahead ... at least, I think. It's hard to tell what's happening. I can make out a clearing, and three figures. One has to be my sister, I think the one on the right. But the other two people are shrouded in fog. Two men. No, wait, one man. The third figure is different from the other two. Yes. It's an animal ... a deer. A stag.

But it's enormous, at least six feet tall at the haunch and a rack of at least twelve feet. Bigger than any animal I could imagine, and dazzlingly white. It is spectacular, the most glorious thing I've ever seen. And then it changes—stag to man. No, back to stag again. Somehow I can't tell the difference in the dark. I can't, won't move. My hands are shaking, and I feel sick.

The shadow gets on her knees and inclines her head, almost as if she were kneeling in the pew. Then she raises her hands, palms upward, waits. The other two pull her to her feet. And now they're all walking together down the clearing, like a bride with one too many grooms. Druids among Neolithic standing stones. Katie's pale hair and teeth are luminescent with laughter. They're singing the sweetest music I ever heard in my whole entire life, better than Katie on the cello, better than any noise on earth or in dreams. The song fills, empties, fills again. It's the stuff of Fair Folk. Or else an angel chorus. I try to speak, to sing, but my voice is gone. I only listen and wish I could join in on this wild hymn. And then, it fades away, deeper and deeper into the forest until they are swallowed up by the mist and the forest is black and blue and silent. A bruise.

The fog is thick and glimmering.

I paw at my eyes and I can't tell what's mist and what's tears. But somehow I know that everything has changed. I'm not going to see Katie again. And now I am terribly, terribly alone, and I feel the knife-twist of my stomach, the gagging hot wretch onto the forest floor, the embrace of the wet earth as my cheek hits the ground, darkness.

The sound of water wakes me just before dawn.

In the green-grey morning light, I stagger to my feet. My head pounds. I take stock.

My hands—red with cold and swollen with scratches. My clothes—earth-stained and damp. I don't know what time it is. Auntie Maeve is supposed to stop by this morning. She'll wonder where I am. Where am I? I can't see our house from here. I'm alone.

No Katie. No anyone. Only questions left.

My throat tastes sour, acrid ... I desperately need to wash my mouth out. Right, yes, the water ... let's find the water. I can hear a stream bubbling nearby, and about fifteen feet past the clearing, I find it. Looks clean enough. The water grips my hands with its fierce cold as I scrub away dirt and thin traces of dried blood. It stings my palms, numbs them. I scoop it up into my mouth, swish, spit, repeat until I can't taste the acid anymore. And then I begin to splash my face, gasping at its iciness, over and over and over again ....

Until something is opening up in me, something clear and sharp and solid, an answer to a question I don't remember asking, and now the sun is breaking the sky open, and its rays pour down the side of the mountain, through the branches, piercing the green-grey veil like the first sunlight from the beginning of time, illuminating the mist, golden, shimmering, alive.

I'll be home soon enough.

But right now, I have only this holy sanctuary, the trees. The stories, the memories.

These things are mine, and mine alone. And I am theirs.

I walk deeper in, and I don't look back.

ON THE BEACH / JACQUELINE SHORTELL-MCSWEENEY

Nobody's Princess

Meg Hurtado Bloom

D tells C to fuck off. She doesn't want to spend her life with somebody who won't really put the past away. She has a lot to do with the future and she can feel that even if nobody else can. She goes home for long enough to pack a bag and then, in the middle of the night when all the reporters are gone, she has her brother drive her to Heathrow where she boards a plane to New York. She refuses to take any money, then or ever. In New York, she nannies for a while, and then she starts to paint. Her paintings are paintings of exile, interrupted attachment, yet possess an inner regality that none can deny, says the NYT. She is offered a show at Tate Modern, and E. attends. They meet. D wears a long-sleeved clinging knit bodycon dress of the finest Italian black wool over a black silk slip. Her hair is black by now (it is the '90s), and the two of them resemble each other more than you would imagine possible. A photo is taken of them at the gallery and published in the T., which hasn't missed the fact that she's an ex. C, too, is stunned. He phones her the next day.

D tells C to fuck off. C is stunned. D goes home and gives everyone the silent treatment for a week. Then she calls up one of her old school friends who's on holiday in Paris. They go shopping at Balmain, stuff themselves with pastry. They get drunk in the Marais and are almost run over by a taxi. D thinks she is going to throw up but then she doesn't. They laugh all the way back to the friend's hotel. In the morning they will stumble around until they find strong coffee and two beautiful boys, the first of many.

D tells C to fuck off. C is stunned. D goes home and locks herself in her room. Nobody can bring themselves to ask what happened. They leave meals outside her room for a month. When it is clear that she has already had a nervous breakdown, she joins the family for meals again. She appears incredibly serene, but doesn't gain any weight. This goes on for another month and then one day her sister finds a note saying that she simply needs to clear her head. They have no idea where she has gone. She has left her little car in the airport parking lot and her father has to have it towed home. A decade later, she returns, the veiled and glowing wife of an Iranian doctor who has recently joined the board of a prominent London health charity. They have two beautiful boys.

D tells C no thank you, and then asks if someone can drive her car home for her, because she isn't feeling well. It is awkward. C is stunned, but sends someone. The press linger outside her father's house for weeks, and everyone feels embarrassed about it. Nobody asks her what happened, they know that D is a very single-minded girl. D tries to go back to work at the nursery school but it is very awkward. D sees a photo of C in the paper with the new princess and feels very sure that she has missed her biggest chance. And then she thinks, Well, what's there to do? She quits her job, even though the press has left her alone for weeks. She asks her father for a tutor and completes her A-levels, enrolls at U, but doesn't do very well, and when she meets a nice boy named R, that's that, they get married. They have two boys. R's mother runs a prominent charity from a chic little office in Chelsea, so D gets a job there, truly makes a difference among the poor of London, and then goes shopping after work. Occasionally people remember that she might have become a princess and didn't. D lives.

D tells C, no thank you. C says nothing, sends her home. She tells her family everything, and they send her to friends in New York. The friends are kind, her family sends her an allowance. She dances again. She makes a whole gaggle of lovely girlfriends, none of whom have any idea where she's coming from. She's happy, but she's lonely. One night her mother's friend says, "Why don't you come to the Met Gala with me? H has the most terrible headache," and she goes. She meets a fluffy-haired tycoon who simply won't leave her alone—eventually, the press outside the house becomes unbearable. She writes to her brother, who has been drinking a lot since she left and decides to lawyer up. She isn't sure, but then runs into the tycoon in the loo at Christie's of all places. What he does there steels her, and she hires three more lawyers the next day, fathers of her girlfriends. They find all kinds of damning tidbits about a man nobody has really noticed yet—but it's enough. D takes half his empire, starts a magazine, a television station, and a training corps for compassionate nannies in the City. D lives. Things change.

D tells C to fuck off. C is stunned. He asks, Are you very sure? She says, Oh, yes. She goes home. But on holiday with The Family she has fallen in love with the Highlands, and she knows what she must do. She asks her father for a job in finance. He is stunned, but finds a way. She works on the London Exchange for three years, wearing navy suits every day. She was nervous at first, because everyone said she wasn't good at maths, but her charm and intuition prove unstoppable on the trading floor. She makes a fortune of her own, buys a little cottage outside Inverness, with a little stone wall to shield the chickens from the icy wind. D likes to have tea in her garden wearing the evening gowns she's had shipped from London. Her neighbors wave and think how good it is to see her. She lives alone, and enjoys a string of male visitors, some of them very young men hired from nearby villages. Her family assumes she has gone mad at last and never speaks to her again. But she has kept up her investments, and has a small army of young women doing her bidding in London, so within another three years she buys the meadow attached to her cottage, and builds a barn, and a little pavilion for picnics. She imports two little Dartmoor ponies, names them W and H, and grants the neighbor children rides whenever they ask.

D tells C to fuck off. C is stunned. D goes home and cleans her room, her sister's room, her brother's room, the library, the kitchen, the back stairs. She enrolls at London College, in the fashion department. She does very well. Her father knows the owner of Harrod's and she grew up with his son, so she gets a job immediately at the head of their styling league. C has waited around and found another prospective princess about whom he feels just the same, and now they're getting married. He comes to D and says, It's no hard feelings, you always had such an eye and Mummy liked you, could you come and dress her for the wedding? D says, of course, and she is thrilled, and picks out a daring full-skirted suit for E which will change everything else E wears for years. The Day-Of, D is on set to handle any last-minute stitchings ... for any other client she could have sent an assistant, but E is notoriously private and knows that D "knows how it works" so would prefer D handle any adjustments (The bride needs the dress taken in, of course.) D frolics with the flower girls and C sees her and how happy she is and he wonders, he definitely wonders. But then C thinks of C and all's well. D was of course already a celebrity stylist of the greatest reach but now that she has dressed the Q she is untouchable. She buys her brother out of the S estate, adopts seven children and employs an army of young refugees as nannies. They will all receive college degrees and a job placement of their dreams. D grows old, surrounded. She wears a lot of red.

My Father Built a Raft

Ron Pullins

My father built a raft.

He built a lot of things. He came back from the war and built a locker plant with rented drawers for freezing food and a slaughterhouse for butchering cattle, hogs. When they tore that old place down, they found its forty years of walls had filled with ice, self-insulated, as igloos are, and quiet.

He dreamed of floating down the local river, a trickle except in flood, flowing from our Flint Hills here in Kansas to the Missouri, then down to New Orleans on the lazy Mississippi.

His raft, barrels soldered into columns and braced by two-by-fours, covered then with plywood that was strong, and added an old motor fueled by gas he had salvaged.

It tired him out, I suppose, those years of slaughtering, cutting throats, the bleeding from the cuts, the creation of bacon, grinding burgers, perhaps the incessant look of hunger on the faces of his customers. This he did in years he spent unknowingly encased in ice, birthing then, I suppose, his long-lingering plan to escape. Down the Mississippi. To New Orleans. With every throat he cut. With every heart extracted.

One summer morning, then, at the local lake, to test the thing, he floats the raft off a makeshift trailer. He stands atop the plywood, then pulls and pulls the motor's rope, and pulls and pulls again, so say they who watch him there, ineffectual effects as his raft drifts out, so say those who happen by, those in support of father's dream, until in the middle of the lake the raft collapses in the center, caves in and takes my father down, who with his motor sinks, and drowns, suicide by dream, as I remember.

The truth is, he didn't drown, of course. The raft collapsed, and he swam ashore, to begin another dream, so I suppose. It was escape that drowned that day, both his and mine. He floats on me on this vast and quiet lake. I will not break under the weight of his regrets.

Hope on the Horizon

/ Lindsey Morrison Grant

Quarterly Editor's Prize

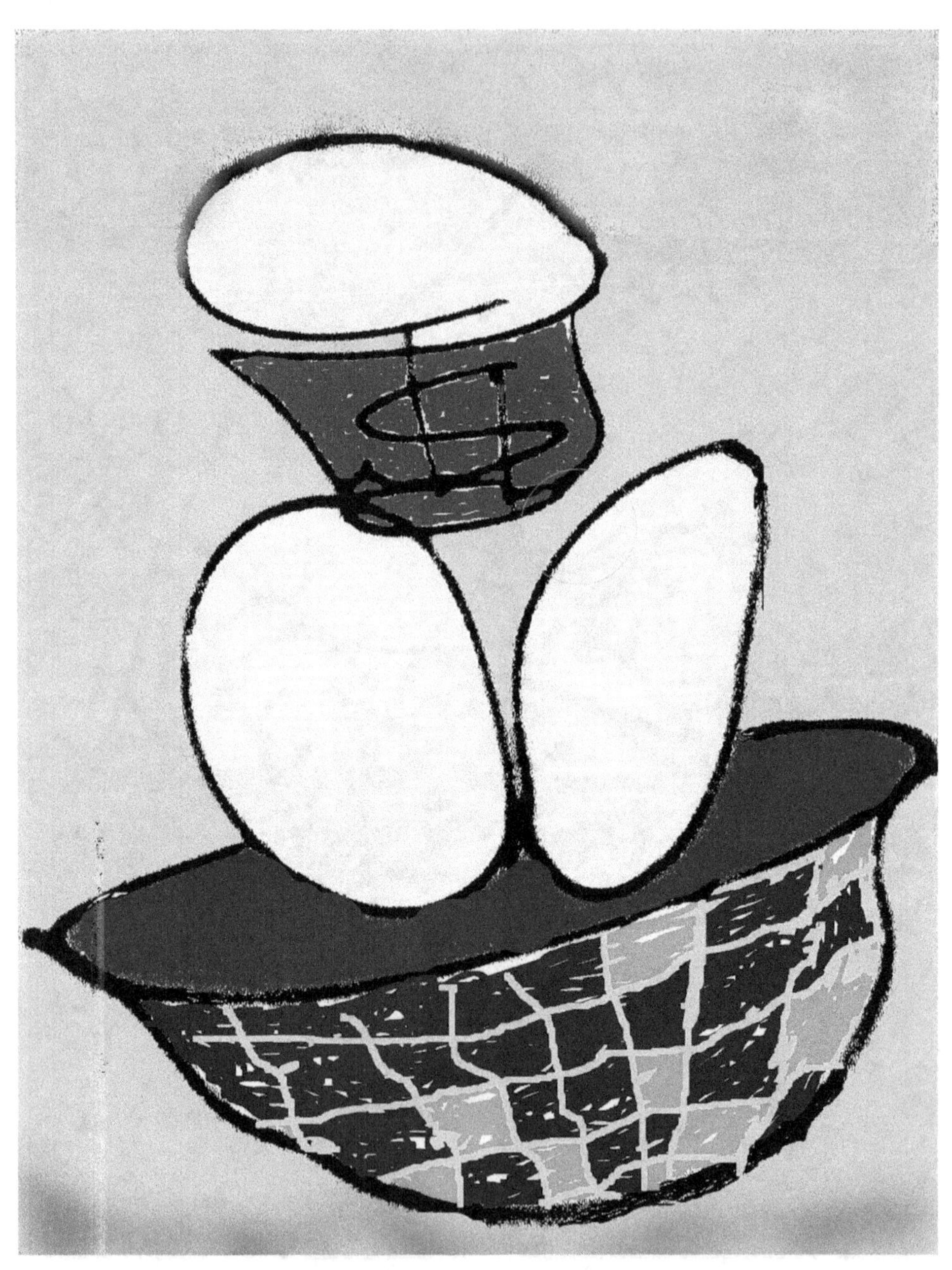

Graffiti Reimagined

/ Linsey Morrison Grant

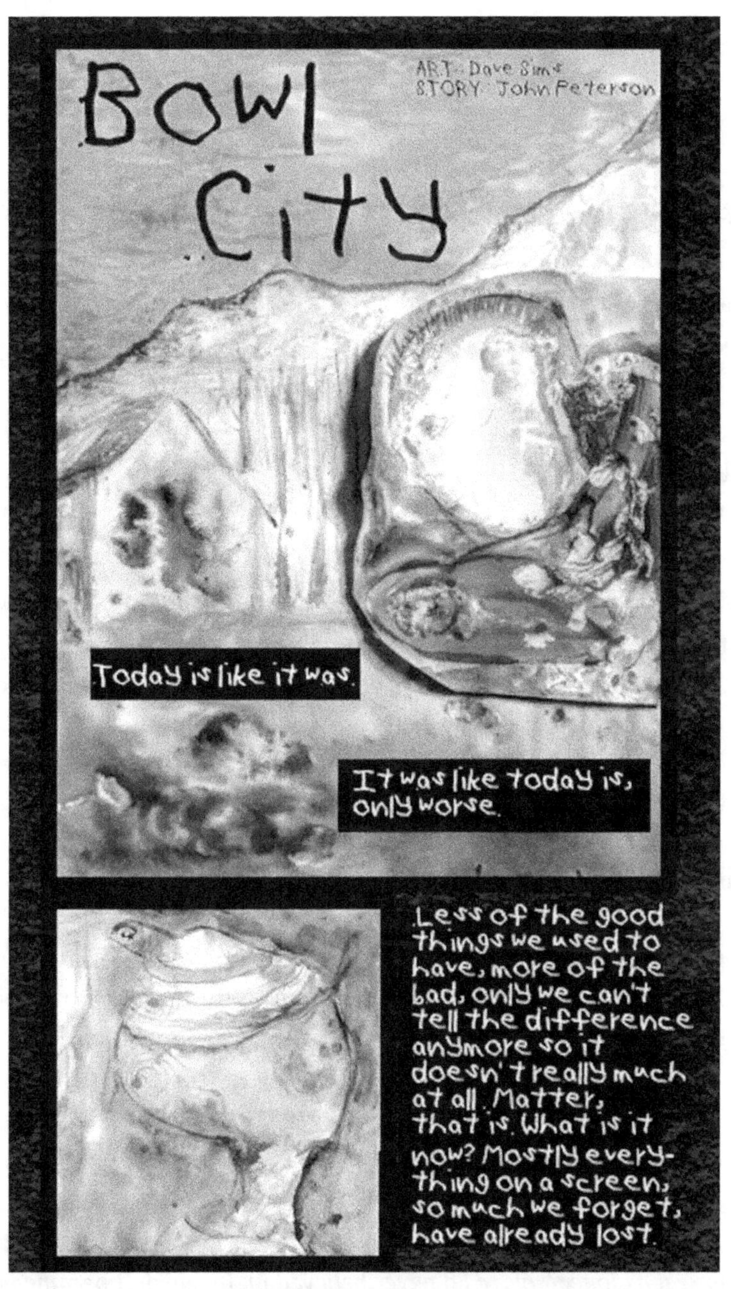

Bowl City Splash Page / Dave Sims

Inception Winner

ORPHEUS FAR FROM THE ABYSS

MEAGAN DAINE

INCEPTION RUNNER-UP

Orpheus. Do you remember when we used to climb the dusty hill and push through tangled thorns to reach the eucalyptus grove? The spicy smell of the trees. The strips of bark, long as we were tall but fragile, easy to take in the fingers and crack to let the fragrance stain the hands. The dry, fallen leaves in the thick grass, the cool grass sometimes parting, sometimes buried beneath them. The grass pushing up in stalks, knots, bunches, finally to hillocks covered in bell-shaped yellow flowers. You taught me to pluck these flowers and chew the stems for their sour juices.

Do you remember?

Orpheus. Sometimes I dream that we are walking up that hill again and I am happy as if my heart were full of sunlight because I know you have forgiven me.

In school I knew a man who wrote strange music. He hunched over the keys of an old piano and played through the night. Tones spilled through the window into the garden where I walked, splashing colors onto my path, painting a world I'd never been able to reach alone. A place I'd never believed in. In which it became impossible not to believe.

This Summer I Hear the Gun

Noah Ruiz

Inception Finalist

First of all, I have three questions for you:

1. Please fill in the blank below.

"Racial hate had been the bane of my life, and here before my eyes was concrete proof that it could be abolished. Yet a new hate had come to take the place of the rankling racial hate. It was irrational that ___ should hate what they called "intellectuals" or anybody who tried to think for himself. I had fled men who did not like the color of my skin, and now I was among men who did not like the tone of my thoughts."

—Richard Wright, writing from Paris, France, 1944.

A. Communists
B. ANTIFA
C. Trump supporters
D. Covid-19 Victims
E. The CDC
F. George Floyd Protesters
G. All of the above

2. Choose the answer below that best defines “2020” as a linguistic neologism (i.e., beyond its literal referent—how is it being used in discourse now, as more than just a number?):

A. The intersection of race, politics, police brutality, pandemic, and economic disaster
B. A statement of moral despair about the state of our culture, our nation, and the world
C. The year I graduated college
D. The third year since I entered college
E. The third consecutive year since I was last brutalized by a member of the police force

3. What Race / Ethnicity are you?

A. White
B. Mexican
C. Both?
D. Culturally white and American, ethnically mixed-race descent
E. None of the above
F. All of the above
G. A and B only

Eye of the Sun / Evelyn M

Inception Finalist

Spiderland

DS Higdon

Inception Finalist

We spent nights in the basement. We shared our space with thin-legged spiders and humpback crickets, minor things that scurried and hugged shadows. Earth wept through the foundation, damp cinderblocks stained with specks of dirt, like blackheads on a shy boy's face. We spent nights under mason jars ranked on plywood shelves, opaque with kraut, pickles, peppers, pole beans, and crushed tomatoes. Behind a bedsheet curtain, Issacs's dad grew pot in five-gallon buckets under fluorescent lights. We strung Christmas lights from the joists and scavenged a stack of 45s from a moldy cardboard box. *One Toke Over the Line Sweet Jesus. Cover of the Rolling Stone.* We flipped through creased *Hustlers* and Swamp Thing comics. The coils of a space heater glowed and hummed in a corner, and we smoked Newports I stole from Mom's purse. We exhaled our dreams from the window well into the cold dark sky, only our faces and the constellations reflected in the casement pane.

NAIADS

JANNA URSCHEL

INCEPTION FINALIST

One wrinkly Naiad after another washed up to shore, crisp and leathery. At first, people mistook them for fish, dried-up fish. But even after they knew better, they figured, why not? Seafood is seafood

No one even knew there were Naiads in the Hudson until they started dying.

"This isn't Greece," someone notable complained in a New York Times editorial, and some smartass wrote a letter to the editor in reply to say, "But there's Troy. And Ithaca."

Why were they here? Had they always been here? The scientists were called in, from Boston, mostly, so they could be objective. But they didn't know a good goddamn about mythology. So they brought in the classicists, but there are, like, thirty-seven translations of Ovid, and then someone had to bring up Homer, so until they could get their declensions worked out, they weren't going to be much help either. A noted physicist said something about dimensions, but it was more opaque than the Ovid translations, so no one paid him much mind.

Ad Lucem Aeternam

HR Harper

Culmination Winner

...

What leaves asks for our surrender.

From this end of the story,
freedom and slavery both overrate us.

I was rowing away from shore anyway.

BLUE MUSTANG; RED ROSE

JEANNE WILKINSON

CULMINATION FINALIST

I hung up the phone feeling dizzy, as if I were looking at life through the wrong end of a telescope. As if the events of the past year had twisted my life into a puzzle whose pieces would never fit into that suburban template where the end picture is you, your spouse, and two-point-three kids in front of a big split-level house on a spotless concrete driveway flanked by a neon-green lawn. But I was no longer a girl from the suburbs and, hmmm, was it mescaline in Golden Gate Park where the trees danced, or LSD at the Pacific shoreline where I found my name written in the sand that made me understand I never would be again?

Either way, I was a stranger in an ordinary land, and going on a date with you seemed, well, impossible. Like we'd be speaking different languages and I had no interest in yours anymore and didn't have the energy to teach you mine. And worse, getting close to me could very possibly twist and warp you into some bizarre, distorted shape, and I didn't want that kind of karma marking my soul. Or yours.

So I'd have to find my own way and you'd have to find yours. I hoped yours would be good because you at the gas station—clutching that red rose in your shining, greasy hand—had been an angel in my life at a moment when I'd badly needed one.

Final Crises

Haylee Millikan

Culmination Finalist

I was once groped   by dissonance,   (—a man among men)
& I gripped him until I felt myself
hemorrhage.

MOTION

NOAH RUIZ

CULMINATION FINALIST

I will try to figure out who my father is. Who he was.

When I was an infant, he competed in martial arts tournaments, spectated by grandmasters. He used to weightlift every day. Before he met my mother, he travelled to Europe to play soccer internationally. He worked for the Viper team of software engineers at Comcast. He lacked an official college degree, but he achieved his dream of becoming a multimillionaire through Bitcoin. He retired at age forty-two. He had three children.

See, that doesn't feel like him at all. Past, present, future. None of it makes sense. How are we talking about the same person?

The landscape streams by. Grass, plains. On the other side, mountains. Sun. I haven't said anything since we got on the highway. The house music is still playing. There's a new thumbnail of a different girl in a skirt. She's teasing her breasts, standing on a rooftop in a black crop top. He's still driving, wearing those sunglasses. I bet they're spotless by now.

I sink further into my chair and lean my head against the window as I peer out. I begin drifting in and out of sleep. My head is so heavy. It bobs around from the motion of the car. At ninety miles an hour we are being pushed forward by the rubber wheels, steel mesh, the driveshaft. Always moving forward, inexorably. All my life, we've been on the move. But we haven't crashed yet. I'm always wondering how.

FOR WANT OF PARCHMENT

CLAUDE CLAYTON SMITH

CULMINATION FINALIST

greater men than Homer, or Chaucer, or Shakespeare
what have they not written
for want of parchment

flitting perspectives and demi-experiences
which never die

Tax Season

Tifara Brown

Geminga Winner

6 million bodies on the ocean floor. Fulani. Colored and cursed. Akan. Counting the cost of our reparations. Wolof.

Compounding daily.

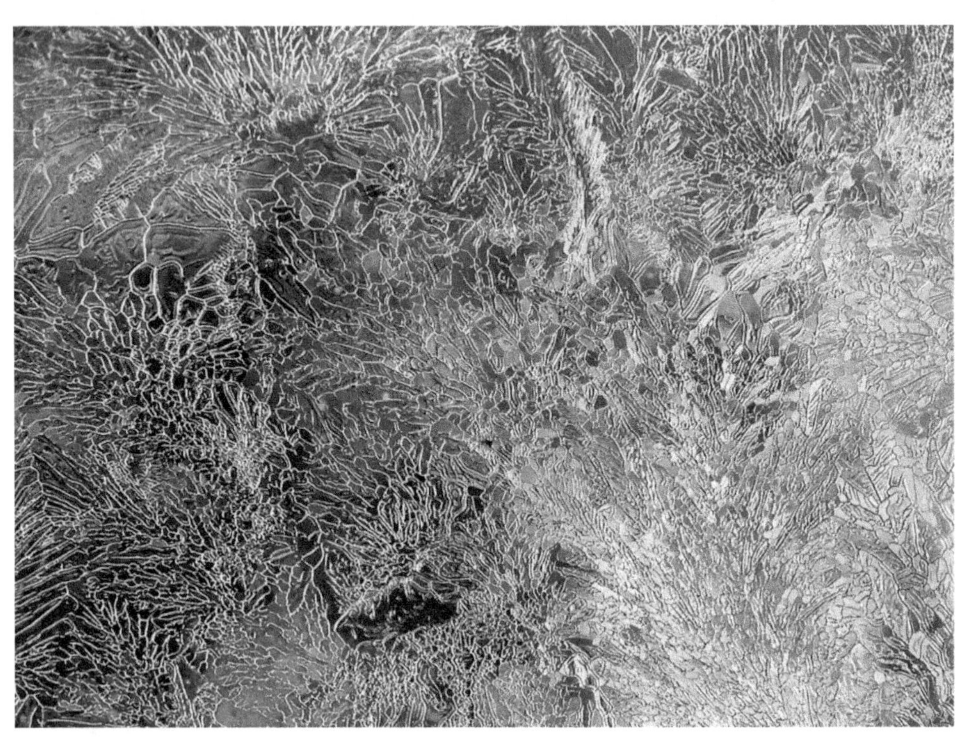

Her Wildest Dreams / Martha Nance

Geminga Runner-Up

KISHIMOTO

RAIN HOU

GEMINGA RUNNER-UP

Kishimoto belongs to the bay, in a knitted dress, willow blue color showing through her palms—hair rolled up as ebb tides. I played her Suite Bergamasque : it sounded like Europe, rhetorically, in my mind, which corresponded with her hands, whispering. The flowering season broke its promise in one night. Only emptiness is stable, with her violin bow changing like a full moon. I named her beloved boy sunflower and connived his name to sprout like a seed. Why the weather cleared up each time I saw him—with sunshine flooding at the back? Flood as a deluge, as an overtone.

Suffers Patiently

JESSICA ROSS

GEMINGA FINALIST

Her parents follow her home from the wake.

"There is a desert in my head," she says. "There is nothing."

Her mother reaches across the table to her. Her mother looks understanding and adoring and, surprisingly, determined.

"There is life in deserts, too," her mother says, stubborn. A child of the playa, hardy and enduring–she makes it sound so simple. "Even there, it endures."

Endures like the unwelcome silence. Endures like the emptiness of her bed. Like the heartache. The quiet.

And she endures like her husband's voice in her memory, reminding her there is life in deserts, too.

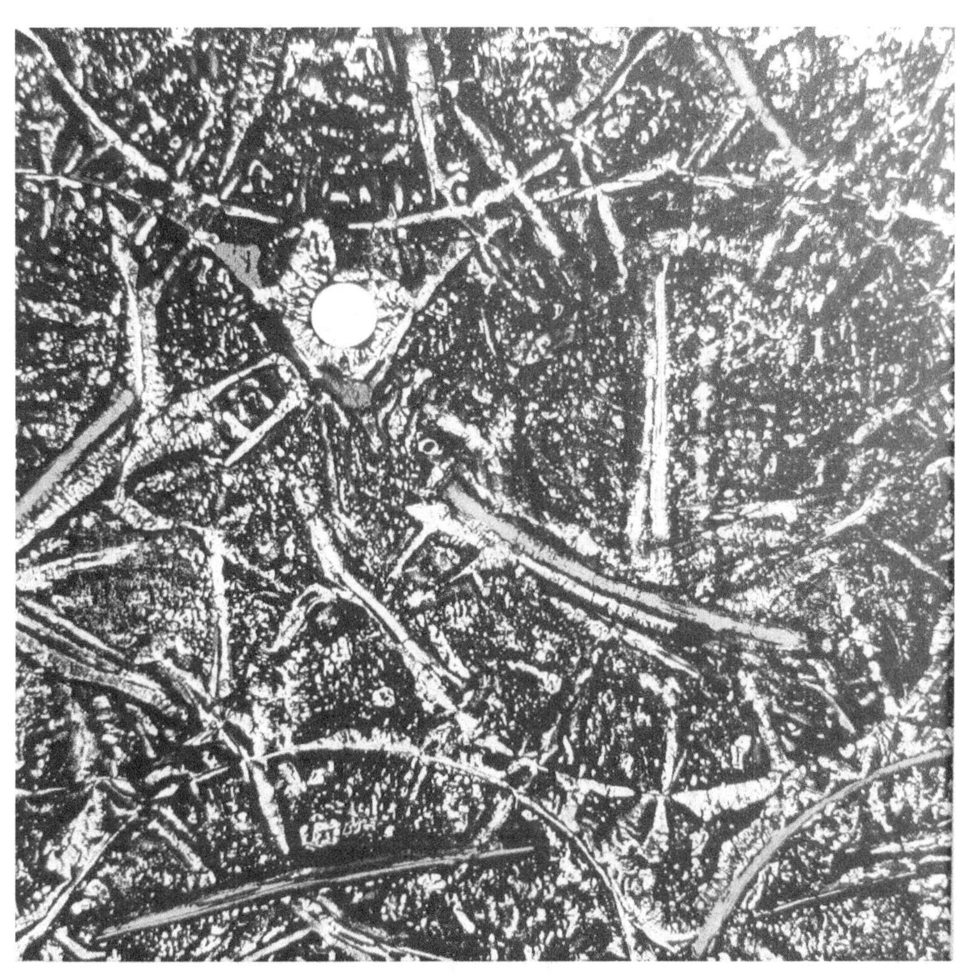

Get All Your Ducks in a Row

/ Pamela Viggiani

Geminga Finalist

Some Days I Can Taste

Atma Frans

Geminga Finalist

the sweet cotton candy
of the one white cloud

floating all on its own
not minding

the lightning popping
and crackling

the storm
moving in on me

Rest Stop, Mile Marker 173

Jen Payne

Geminga Finalist

The Garden State Parkway rest stop was halfway to my grandmother's. We'd pull off the exit and shuffle into the rose-colored stalls of the Ladies Room.

Inside, near the pink-vinyl couch, a pull-knob vending machine sold hairnets, bobby pins, and rainhats neatly folded into pastel plastic boxes.

The rest stop burned down in '91, years after we'd stop traveling as a family. But in my mind, it's all still there—the soft golden light and tiled floors, the vending machine, my sister sleeping, Dad singing "*I Got You Babe*" to Mom in the front seat, his hand on her knee.

ANALOGY

JJ CHEN HENDERSON

GEMINGA FINALIST

In this world, love
has no analogy.
Then why,
as I break
a rhizome
of lotus root,
its lake-mud-
smeared hollows
remind me
of the blanks
in my aging mother's
eyes?

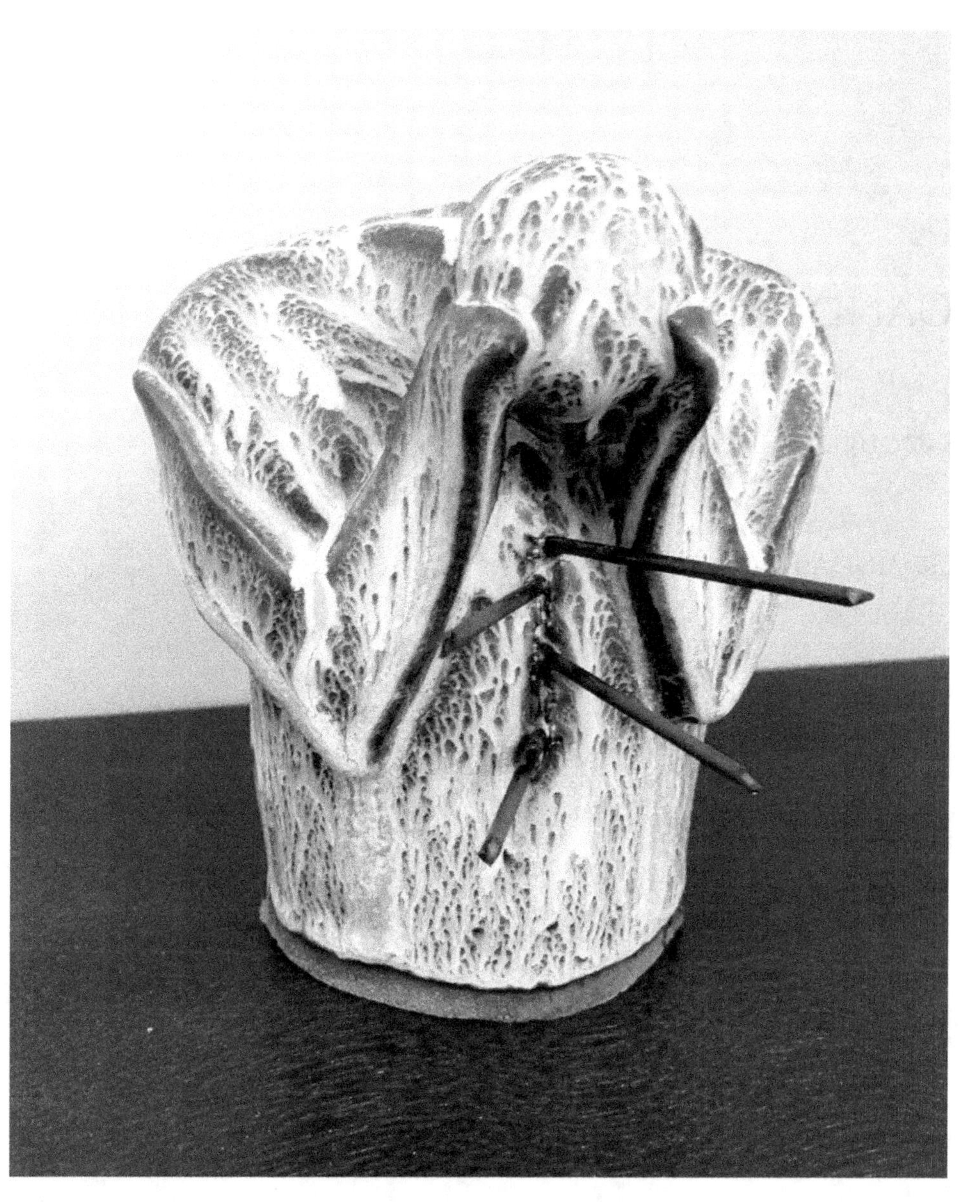

Broken Heart / Paul Milligan

Geminga Finalist

Candy Crush

Jacqueline Schaalje

Geminga Finalist

There was that bf who killed his avatar
with a tear in his pc cooling water.
He drank tea with my parents
and daubed my tongue in candy crush.

Fall Tanka

Sarah Kersey

Geminga Finalist

In between frosts, leaves
sweat, dampen the dying grass.
I almost forget.
Nothing lasts and everything
aches: like a wet metronome.

Only Water

Julie Esther Fisher

Rigel 2022 Winner

She would sometimes bring him food in the tub. Feed him with her naked arms. He splashed around in the water, eating a cream puff, her hand spooning it into his mouth, a migrating finger on his chest if he spilled.

His mother had just sudsed up the tub. Rainbow bubbles stood on the surface and he splashed them, poked them, watched them fly upwards and drift back down. His mouth was filled with small white first teeth. He had not yet been washed, the water was pristine, and the woman with her large hands leaned over the rim of the tub that separated them. He caught hold of a bubble and held it on his outstretched palm with a mouth and eyes of delight. He held the bubble out and slid it on to her palm. It slid on its little river of what flowed from him to her, easy, without resistance, and stood there quivering.

"Gloria, kindly tell me what is the meaning of this?"

His father: arid, his voice the clack of two dry bones.

He brought an envelope out of his pocket and handed it to her.

"He won?" she said. "My boy won the Ivory Soap competition? His face will be on every billboard between here and San Francisco."

His father cracked his knuckles.

"Gloria, you have lowered us. Made us common. People will say we needed the money. You've brought shame on us."

"But look at him. Look at your son, Henry—that face."

"We'll write to them. Tell them we changed our minds." He shoved paper and pen at her. "Take it down, Gloria—Dear Sir—"

"It's too late, Henry. Didn't you read it? The billboards are already in production. It says so here."

She put down the pen and paper, turned toward the tub.

"You're playing a game with the soap?" she said to the little boy.

Beaming, she held out a cream puff.

"Put that down," his father said. "Put it in the bath." He too looked at the boy. "Now eat it."

"But there's soap in there, Henry."

"Then let him eat that, too."

"Henry, please—"

"You're turning him into a Jew sissy."

He stood there. Stern. Seething. Knuckle-cracking.

His mother leaned over and when she and the boy rubbed noses her bosom hung inches from his nose. He gazed deep into the crevasse. The sight of it wet some strange appetite. His mother fed him, delighting in the act that contravened her husband.

Now, in other humid vapors, the grown man Clifford wants to melt the fat from his bones. To become that boy. A bubble-producing sack of happy skin in a room of twos. Two breasts perched on the tub rim. Two hands slapping the water, sending bubbles airborne. Two pairs of eyes to see it all: the bar of soap sliding around the back of him, brushing by his buttocks, slipping between his legs. Ivory soap. *His* soap. He thinks of the little face with its halo of curls on all the billboards. The three of them saw it everywhere, and each time his father looked away, his face screwed with fury.

The memory is lodged somewhere in Clifford's fat, if only he could feel himself beneath it all, beneath the tire rings around his belly.

Profiteroles sit on the side of the tub. He dips a foot in, holding on to the metal bar. Tears squeeze from his eyes.

The last bath. Alone . . .

He'd known women. Asked them each, to a one, to step into his mother's shoes. Never wanted sex with them. Only wanted the water, the washing hand, the food, the glittering eyes that drank him in.

He gazes over his blubber, trying to join these sights with the little boy that still splashes within him. He loves that boy. Or does he just love *being* that boy? There's a difference, he tells himself. No matter how big he got, he was never big enough to fill that bath alone.

Cream puffs? In the tub?

In the warm water the cream floated, the same color as the soap.

Sweet. Bitter.

"Never let anyone see you like this," she said, smothering him in a towel and pressing him to her breast. "Don't cry now." She pushed him from her and gazed at him with eyes as calculating as a shark's. "You're my beautiful boy. You won. You're my winner. My Ivory Soap baby."

He *had* cried, but it felt good. Good to eat the food, the sloppy mess slithering out the gaps between his few tiny teeth, the swallowing gulps between the gasps that shook his body. He didn't know why it should feel good when he was doing something so horrible, when the tastes had gone from sweet to bitter, scouring the insides of his mouth. They were both still here. His father as tall and rigid as a telephone pole, she kneeling, pink and dimpled with mystery in places that his seeing made him shudder. What they shared was as dangerous as the journey of that single bubble he had passed from his palm to hers. A covenant. Theirs alone. His body could feed her too.

Humidity. Steam. Taps on full. Memory pouring out.

His last day here in the Squire Hotel. Too dangerous for such a beast to get into the tub. This is what he tells himself, though he's been eyeing it all week, feeling the bubbling up of some glorious ache he's been harboring all these years. The bathtub? At the sight of it the strange pain pulls at him.

His father hid a stash of Playboys under the bed.

What was wrong with Her—she, who hung over the side of the tub? He, the little boy, looked in these magazines, poured over them, yet was there a single woman as beautiful as she?

At the foot of the mountain of his tummy, his dangly lies slumbering. He can barely feel it—this part of himself—and cannot see it for what lies in its way. But he recollects the stirrings from long ago that warmed the creature from its hibernation. He feels these vague stirrings now.

It happens by accident, the food coming to the wrong room—the sweets trolley clattering with silver platters of profiteroles, strudel, gateaux. The knock comes out of the blue. The trolley is wheeled in and Clifford, thrusting his hand into his pocket for a few bills, thanks the boy and closes the door. A moment later he calls the boy back. He looks deep into the boy's solemn eyes.

"I didn't order this," he says. "There's been a mistake—but then, I don't believe in mistakes. Do you know that when I was a little boy. . ." He looks straight at the boy, who shifts awkwardly. Occupational hazard, Clifford imagines, entering guests' rooms, listening to their ravings. You must hear the strangest things.

"I'm sorry, son, I'm making you uncomfortable. I just need to tell someone . . ."

He looks more probingly at the boy—at his face, his skin.

"How old are you, son?"

"Sixteen, Sir."

Clifford's eyes linger on his. "Nobody's sixteen. Sixteen is a fiction—an impossibility . . ." He shakes his head. "Do you know that when I was your age—"

He's been drinking and yes, he *is* a little drunk.

"—I was beautiful. Such a beautiful boy. I don't know what . . ."

He indicates his present body and starts to leak tears. So help him, he is bawling his eyes out. He can see the boy wondering whether the tips will be worth it.

Pointing to the sweets trolley, Clifford says, "You see that? You see what's on there? You want to eat sweets, but sometimes you can't. Sometimes you just have to eat...soap."

In the silence, the sound of the tub filling.

"Do you have any idea how hard it is for a man like me to get clean? How dangerous it is? Do me a favor, son. Stay with me. Make sure I come out. I don't want to be alone. I need to fix myself up. I have a big day tomorrow."

He is spewing tears.

Mother and son play with the bar of soap in the tub. He tries to catch it. She sends it up between his legs. Oh, but it tickled his dangly, as she called it. Now she was reaching in there and his eyes were wide with delight, her fingers brushing by it. They laughed. He did not know what delighted him exactly—bubbles, soap, food, breasts, laughter, the humid atmosphere? It was a puzzle. What sent his father in? A cold gush of air cutting through the dense intimacy. His father interposed between them. She got up. Not immediately. Not at first.

His father never sets foot in here. He is always out there, chair bound, reading his newspaper, smoking his pipe, pretending not to think of his stashed magazines. So why does he come in now and talk to her so gruffly? Why does his father look at him with such disdain? His skin hurts when his father looks at him. A fire in his father's eyes incinerates everything. Not even this water can put it out. Poor boy. She feeds him, but he is her meal. With every word, look, touch, he knows this at two, three, knows it more surely than something known at twenty, thirty, sixty, seventy. He wanted to say Daddy get me out of here. His father—God, how he loved the man for making him eat soap!

"Do me a favor, son," Clifford says to the room service boy. "Stay here till I get out. There's dosh in it. Lots."

"But, Sir, there's all the other rooms to serve. And Mr. Carter, he'll have my guts for—"

"Life is full of Mr. Carters, son. I need you more than he does."

Looking askance at Clifford, the boy says, "You ain't gonna slit your wrists in there, are you?"

"No." Clifford smiles ruefully.

They are silent a moment. Then the boy says, “Mr. Carter. He’s very particular. Last year he won room service of the year award.”

Clifford nods. “Once, a long time ago, I won something, too.”

“Cool,” the boy says breezily. “What?”

“What, indeed. That’s the question.”

And now he steps into the bathtub, and the hulk of him, naked and quivering, stands here, afraid to lower himself in.

He looks over his body. Wave upon wave of the flesh that is him. Or is it? He can see the little boy, feel him here, flailing in the torrent. Save me, he calls. Or does he? No, worse, he says nothing. He is flat now, a photograph...no more.

The tub is filling up, yet he dare not do more than sit naked on its edge, holding on, his toe swirling the contents so that the waves spanking the sides fill him with a kind of aching delight. He remembers that she used to do this, though with her hand, swirl the water and they would play a game of find the soap. He remembers with the same aching delight the perfect diamond-ringed hand moving through the steam and coming toward him, coming down in slow motion, as if she were conscious of another layer of meaning that now required this agonizing slowness when all he wanted to do was get on with the game. He would never forget that hand, his anger and disgust for the betraying slowness of its journey. Diamonds sparkled on the polished fingers. And when the hand broke the surface of the water, he was aware of a certain feeling of corruption. She swirled the water, thinking it would delight him, sending the Ivory soap slipping off between his legs and away. He slapped the water, this time not in delight, but in wordless indignation.

“Now, now, Cliffy, don’t make a fuss.”

Only the little hands could express the desolation at the turn in the water, the bittering of something sweet that no perfume of hers could cover up. She leaned in. He brought his knees up to his chest and curled his back, depriving her of a view of his anchor. He didn’t know why he did this, hid the birthmark, clearly it displeased her. He felt that they were both floating now, in peril, without destination. That was when his father came in. The

Ivory was lost somewhere in the water. Yes, he *would* eat soap! Oh, how he wanted to! *Let* him wash his mouth out! Let him digest it! Undo the corruption, the loss. And somehow his father knew. Knew that he'd saved the boy. He couldn't stand this—it wasn't what he meant—*hadn't* been when he marched into the bathroom and demanded to know "the meaning of this."

Her hand crept up his back.

"Baby. Baby boy. Winner. Let me wash you."

Wriggling away. It's a game? Why did he feel afraid?

Smiling of the pink lips. She laughs again.

But he knows this is a warning.

What's threatened? Why should he not wriggle away from the silver cascade she makes so hot? It hurts him! And her hand? Something scrubs his back. An alligator?

"When you are clean," she says, "you can have this." She holds up a fat cream puff. "Don't cry, Mama's little boy. What do you have to cry about? You're a winner."

Something is gone when the room clears. Like returning from a dream—bad or good, he cannot tell. He only knows that it is done — something, done. Is he crying only because it was so hot?

They agree on that reason.

The anchor is stamped on him. She draws her hand across it. Knives of pleasure slice through him.

He wees into the tub, holds on to the soap. She swirls her fingers in the water, creating what vortex into which he'll be sucked if he looks up at her now, laughs, does anything to delight her.

"Don't leave," Clifford calls out to the boy waiting in the bedroom. "Not much longer now."

Taps, tears, time—all run together.

Then comes the voice.

"Sir, are you all right?"

Clifford stands dripping over the bathroom floor.

"Don't worry, son, you'll soon have your dosh."

"It isn't that, Sir. . ."

The door opens. Tears jump from Clifford's eyes. The boy's eyes widen with shock and horror at the sight of the quivering flesh. In spite of themselves, they rove over the body as eyes do at sight of a ghastly accident.

He knows that the boy will never forget this moment. Never forget it because he will never understand it. He feels sorry now for using him, for frightening him, confusing him.

"I wasn't always this way," he says gently, letting the bar of soap slip from his hand. "I'm sorry. I'm frightening you. I'll cover myself up."

A towel hangs from the dripping arm, but it is too small— what part of himself should he cover up? The chest with its fabulous tits, his belly that is not one but the rippling waves of many, or the wan genitalia that hang lifeless underneath. Useless. The boy has seen it all.

Clifford says, "Tonight I've subjected you to something you'll never forget. But I want to tell you why. You should at least know why."

He knows that the boy waits and that his waiting is like the waiting for an ambulance after an accident. He wonders what to say? How to explain?

At length, he walks to the edge of the bed and sits down. He can feel the boy's eyes on him, rapt, bewildered.

"I want to tell you why, but I don't know how," he says simply.

The boy walks over to where the soap lies on the floor and picks it up. He doesn't know what he holds—doesn't know the meaning of it to the man who's dropped it, but it is a tender gesture from one so scared, it takes courage, like picking up some personal effect from the asphalt after the body's been thrown from the car.

"I knew who I was once. For a little while . . . I wasn't always like this. People didn't always look at me—the way you're looking at me now. Once—"

The boy lowers his eyes.

"No, no, son, don't look away . . . Once... But that was a long time ago now . . . If it wasn't for a picture—a single photograph taken long ago—I'd never believe it possible either. I'm trying to explain it to you," Clifford says when the boy looks up. "Because boys understand. But boys become men. And then they stop."

Afraid he might cry again, he lowers his eyes. He knows he has the boy's attention, totally and without qualification. He knows that something is happening between them. He knows that the boy feels it, too—feels that they have passed from some weird, potentially vulgar encounter to something mysterious, a story—something he might still be telling years from now.

Sometimes big things happen to little people and little things happen to big people. The thing is, sometimes the big people *are* the little people.

Now the boy walks over and covers the shivering body with the blanket he pulls from the bed. But it is the boy's presence that wraps Clifford in warmth. The fact that he is still here. Stays. Doesn't run away.

"I've wet your floor," is all Clifford can think to say.

"It's your floor, Sir," the boy replies. "Your room." He looks Clifford right in the eye. "But not to worry. It's only water."

Kearney Noir / Larry Hill

Rigel 2022 Runner-Up

Santa Corona

Michael Pearce

Rigel 2022 Runner-Up

1.

Sailing on my bicycle, my silent chariot,
along streets my bike knows, has been
a hundred times
                    but they're different now
their colors are brighter
their quiet quieter and
the vigilant families that walk them
glide by in crystal bubbles,
I swerve wide arcs, speak soft hellos
so as not to shatter . . .

these are not the same streets.

Familiar smells hang in the air we plunge through—
the smoke of grilling beef
the harsh perfume of fabric softeners
the exhaust of a diesel 18-wheeler
the pungent stink of frying fish
the simmer of tomato-plantain-sausage-yucca
the pitchy fragrance of fresh-cut fir—
familiar smells now drawn with effort
through a mask infused with the chlorine and sulfur
of paper and the dank sour of my breath.

An old couple on the sidewalk,
dark freckly faces on the move
step lightly as if they were barefoot,
and they are quiet, too intent to smile or nod,
unlike the nearby parents and kids.
I see them through your eyes now
needless martyr (obscure and ubiquitous
tragic and foolhardy and absurd)
I see fragile lives, shaky as fall leaves,
matchflames under torn umbrellas
I see . . .
          I'm not sure what I see
I try to see what's there and then some.

          2.
You can't see dead saints, they are
a presence close and intent
you wonder if that ripple of shame
or clarity is their celestial breath.
A dark shimmer, a silent crackle
that animates the air around you
they arrive without summons
loiter with smug abandon
your prayers spread you open
like butchered meat you become
their ward, their project, their prey.

Santa Corona is in the neighborhood,
a floral bloom, a waxy reptile scent,
an expectation as before a ballgame
or concert, she has no dimension
but in a crowd, among the buzz
and titter, she is the bond and
roar she is the worry and awe.

Spirit and breath that animates,
infectious smile, choral amen,
exhalation of promise of resolve
of resignation of compassion,
a slow, anxious pant, a steer in
a chute, not quite choosing
where to go but going calmly
and with a timeless comfort:
you can't see viruses or dead saints.

3.

Drawn to the chicken factory
the prison the old folks' home
the mortuary the clinic the hospital
drawn to the tomato sorter
the handler of meat mail fruit garbage
cash plastic bags and boxes
to the hands the eyes the mouth
the breathing lungs of the handler
to the husband the children
the parents the friends of the handler
I sidle to   snuggle with   shudder
under hands warm and sticky with
the thick juice of desire
oh people!
            people you are my destiny
my calling my happy medium.

Drawn to the west side of town
the tall tenements the sturdy bungalows
of faded paint and spike iron fences
sounds of Tupac Lauren Wu-Tang
spill from grated windows
defiance in a pumping meter
you exhale a martyr's affinity

for the tired, the hungry, the homeless
yearning to breathe free
knowing the blue flame under
that cliché is pestilence the terror
of pestilence the vigor the hunger of
insatiable submicro purpose
gone global gone
hostile gone takeover.

Drawn to the teaming beach
the sports arena the nightclub
the concert hall the restaurant
the slow parade the ardent protest
she is in the air she sticks around
awhile maybe longer maybe
migrates to another fertile field
another undawn in the overbelly
billowy bags she inspires she
incites to riotous fever pitch
she consumes with an untropy
that is beyond passion.

4.

I don't remember when she first arrived,
I wasn't home maybe, or slept,
or yanked the front door open to
receive a package. Maybe Grace,
my kid, snuck her in when I
was in the shower. She lives here now.

Lives and whispers, runs barefoot
round the block, dances on
the kitchen table, chews my sweets
mouth wide open
files my nails with a calloused sole,

takes off her mask and tells her story
with a salesman's wink and shake,
she's here until the experts say she's gone

and then she's here again.

5.

Don't touch me stranger
don't cross that line
your gifts are gift horses
your food is tainted
you people smell bad
clothe your face
remove your shoes
she has a stained aura
disinfect with holy water
quarantine at Ellis Island
you chinks with your flu
you wops with your diseases
you kikes you niggers you faggots
you huddled masses when
I touch what you have touched
I feel a fine damp dust spread awhirl
from my fingertips I feel
a tingling in my blood
this simmer in my lungs
takes on a grim weight

6.

My domain has expanded
to every corner of your life
my genome shed in pernicious bits
we enter the air you breathe your home
your water your conversations
your routines your eating habits

your tentative gait the way
you meet talk love sob
every ache cough sneeze worry
pulls you home to me

7.

I am a vacuum
I inhale I devour I plunder
I prey I dismember I consume
I engorge I digest and shit big
I contain lies that suck out
the valor of honesty
the balm of kindness
the leveling of facts
I contain the absence
of empathy generosity
compassion simple pity.

You elected me you can't
escape my words my decrees
every fart from my mouth
goes viral every twitch of my
infectious prick breeds pain
every tick contagious
every action murderous
I luxuriate in such fetid slime
without containment
I am communicable
I contaminate multitudes.

8.

Underneath her laugh
another tireless voice keens
a new life burning.

9.

Who are you?
Italian, they say, married
to a Roman soldier
tromping through Syria
a century after your so-called savior.
A crypto-Christian who they say rushed
to comfort a Christian martyr
and plunged into the demented cruelty
that Romans visited on Christians
that Roman Christians visited on
the rest of us Jews Huns Mongols
heathens heretics scientists.
A teenage girl, they say, cursed
with passionate empathy
precursing martyrs of all stripes . . .
Who are you?

10.

Trillions of us and then some
you better learn our ways

You figured me out, farmgirl,
sorted grain and pulse you
cultivated like crazy
sniffing and sifting for
sugar starch and crumby bulk
you couldn't see the math
but found the method
unlocked the vault of my bounty
the gate to your majestic city

I'm the skinny one
if you want them melonic cells
go north I'm a red chili pepper

can you feel this tiny allele
this micro-cuz come to steal
thunder from that buzzy
mal-aerial bloodbug but hey
don't thank me from the
bottom of your anemic heart
this skinny sicko guy aint
so hale it aint all good baby
but it good enough
you *feel* me?

We find our way we adapt
we're in it for us and no
one else it's on you to figure
two and two then dash
like a sprinter with dense shins
and fast-twitch thighs
you're up against time and
multitudes that don't care

Trillions of us and then some
survive by sifting the shifting
codes the stubborn mutant chunks
that twist and claw from freak
to function to fiddle fight and
fuck   you   up

11.

The cool green-blue that clothes us
masks danger tedium dead sweat
the cruel math of risk . . .

The dry airy pulse of machine
that is your lung for now
your-last-breath, your-last-breath . . .

Automobiles, each its own cell
waiting dully hummly for some
dumb thing to climb inside . . .

Triage in parking lot tents
beds counted and coveted
bagged bodies stacked like sheaves . . .

A life saved and delivered
horizontal on its gurney limo
a wan smile to tired applause . . .

My chest, that chamber that refreshed
without effort, now boils hacks burns
in chronic sighs, *sus*-pir, *sussss*-pirrr . . .

My head the center of gather input
decipher intend respond control
now throbs boils grinds me big . . .

Tough fist crams hard plastic tube
through choking throat into chest
that burns struggles acquiesces . . .

He calls himself a long-hauler
you call yourself fighter
the press of time knows better . . .

My self contracts around me
some days beyond exhaustion
sometimes your body is your soul . . .

12.

Cars hum, trucks groan, bicycles slither,
we walk past the bakery the drugstore
the dead movie theater walk into
the market with its onions and oranges
its rice and beans chicken and broccoli
bread milk beer toilet paper
its invisible clouds of pregnant droplets
its workers basking in nasty air
some have left, most are still there for us.

You don't breathe like you used to
or smell or taste or step or think
you've been somewhere I haven't
maybe you have a story maybe
you survived with nothing to say.
Maybe we stand, a rotten fence between us
one of us hacking and aching in
this warm room on that frozen street.

Those old men and women waiting
in line, murmuring — have they been spared?
That package deliverer that chicken slaughterer
that short-order cook that hospital orderly
that old cop that grocery checker —
guess who's been granted immunity
or bought it for thirty shares of Amazon
guess how safe that makes them
guess when your turn will come
your turn to wheeze, boil, choke, croak,
your turn to savor the fruits of science
the exorbitant gift that zooms in close
plucks snippets of code the itty bitty bugs
that fiddle with your micro nuts and bolts
and make decisions final.

There is history and there is forgetting
and here we stand, masters of both—
ride this littered road that leads
everywhere including a future without
the choke of contagion with only a smoky
memory of an orange and black masque.
Maybe we're a peloton each hugging close
to the one in front yet trying not to kiss
that spinning wheel . . .
                                        never trust
metaphors about love or death.

She walks these streets not like a saint
we're talking something else here
her words follow the rhythm of her breathing
and of her stubborn steps and
history is the story of our infectious
love of ourselves, each other,
                                                    we inhale.

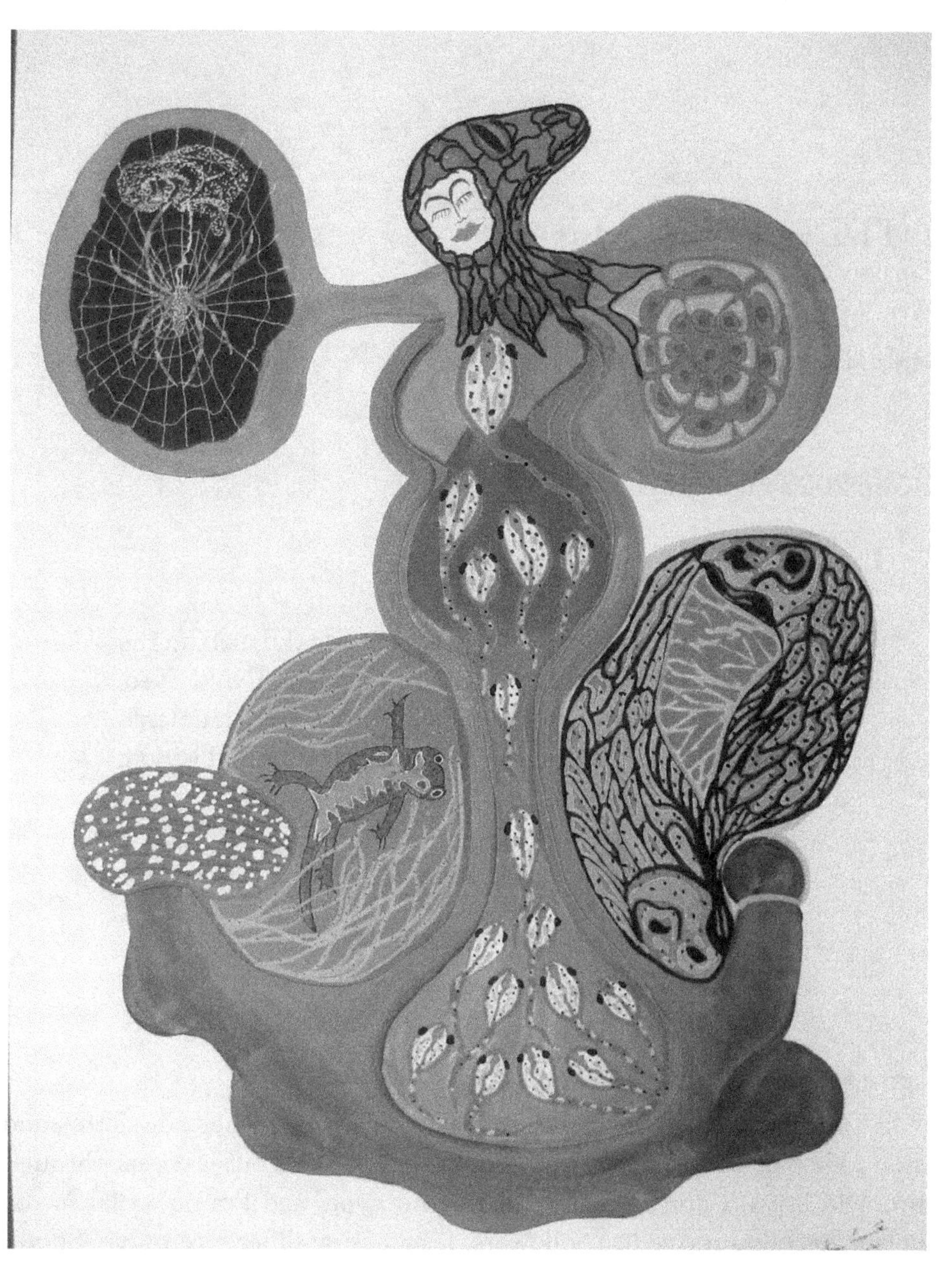

THE WEAVER / SERGE LECOMTE

RIGEL 2022 FINALIST

WITCH OF WALS

BRYAN EDENFIELD

RIGEL 2022 FINALIST

> For some reason it has not trickled down to the man on the street that some physicists now are a bunch of wild-eyed, raving mystics. For they have perfected their instruments and methods just enough to whisk away the crucial venom and what stands revealed is the Cheshire's grin.
>
> — Annie Dillard, *Pilgrim at Tinker Creek*

FIRE

I am a follower of the Witch of Wals.

I follow her on all the platforms. I subscribe to her newsletter and listen to her podcast. I bought her book when it came out last year through Chronicle Press. I don't usually fall for the hype, and I'm no social media maven. 40 Followers; 40,000 Followers: it makes no difference to me. I don't know an Influencer from a Flux Capacitor and can't tell my tweets from my toks. I'm not tech illiterate—my Office skills are topnotch—but the faces in my book are mostly default purple.

Maybe that's why she appeals to me. No one notices me. I've spent four decades cultivating invisibility. If I had the nerve, I'd make an excellent thief, but I lack the burning desire for danger. Give me nerve, please. Send a charge through my inert body. I don't mind if you charge for the charge; that only makes sense, considering the first law of thermodynamics. My credit is a vision of the future. But I can't feel my skin sometimes. The world glosses over me like a featureless thing, less than a breeze. I'm not quite numb—I can feel temperature, pressure—but certain tactile qualities allude me, the timbre of texture muted. Where is that vibrancy of life I hear so much about?

The Witch of Wals asks these same questions.

She has only 20.8 million followers online. She follows 4; I haven't bothered to see who. On a planet of nearly 8 billion people, 20.8 million equals only about one quarter of one percent of the whole. How much influence can she really have? That's less than the population of Beijing but very slightly more than the population of the New York metropolitan area. But her reach goes beyond her followers. Many of those 20.8 million people worship her fervently and share her teachings with messianic urgency. Even if that were not the case, would it matter? The 26 richest people in the world own as much as 3.8 billion poor people. Does it matter if a house cleaner in Kolkata knows nothing of the Witch, when prominent and wealthy entertainment moguls spread her gospel?

I'm not sure how I stumbled onto her work. The algorithm, right? The flow of energy harnessed and redirected via binary code. One has to wonder if the algorithm now aligns with god's will, syncs with the moral arc of the universe. Originally, they designed it to channel propagandistic content—ads, or worldviews—to those most likely to respond to it. That response need not be positive. We either swallow it or negatively react to it in a way beneficial to the status quo; either way, we do what they want. But over time, maybe the algorithm's logic evolves away from capitalism and towards a different cult of mystery.

It is a mystery cult, isn't it, the Cult of Capitalism? We're all prey to its whims, but only a select few are initiated into the inner sanctum, their status achieved by right of lineage. Occasionally, new money is admitted due to perhaps low birthrates amongst industrialized countries. I don't know; I'm just spitballin'. I don't fault Capitalism for aspiring toward spiritual status; it never made sense as a rational philosophy anyway. Fittingly, one wonders if this introduces a Hegelian antithesis into the supposed enlightened secularism of liberal economic ideology. If we worship mystery, how can our allegiance to a self-flagellating series of rules founded on rational certainty make any sense? That'd be sacrilegious! The professional Capitalist, pretending as if he didn't know, makes no claim that his sacred path is a path of mystery, but that's because he was born into the Inner Sanctum and to him sacred knowledge is banal. That doesn't seem like how a mystery cult should work. Maybe I've got this all wrong. Moving on.

My point here is that I'm perhaps not the kind of person that you'd peg for a follower of the Witch of Wals. But I am. And I'm going to go see her tomorrow.

EARTH

She's stationed near the produce, but accessible only via Aisle 9: Bath and Body. Her location ascribes to disobedient physics. To enter the cave, ascend the silver and black escalators towards the blue neon lights. There, you are greeted by an elder clad in blue robes. He ushers you toward avenues of sacrifice and bounty: a pound of my flesh, my labor, for a dozen rolls of paper towels. The busy sun beats down on the earth a frenzied energy, and the earth takes the fire and turns it into life. We dig into the earth and turn it back into fire: see it there on the walls sparkling; see it in your very own hands, buzzing and chiming; see it blinking across the skyline. We swallow the earth. With the energy, we grow food, we eat it, we swallow it more.

I wander through the illuminated valley, the procession of vegetables glittering beneath a constant spritzing of water vapor. I can't even comprehend the energy we've poured into this lettuce. The human body aches to transform the earth so that it may produce this lettuce. Our machines, our chemical inventions, manipulate the genomic composition of this lettuce, maybe. Our chemicals keep the pastures clean, chemicals forged in the fire of the earth, from the wet life of the earth.

These are the teachings of the Witch of Wals. There is no better home for her than here, amongst the products of the assembly line. Beyond, in a different indoor biome marked by dimmer lights and carpeted floors, home goods beckon, arranged in simulation of the Middle-American home. A chant drones over loudspeakers, a folk tune of static thumping weight, a real pop banger structured chorus chorus chorus chorus. What's this idol's name? It's on the tip of my tongue . . .

Just as I think I've remembered, a priest's voice booms with a subdued crackle and speaks in tongues a command that only the initiated can understand.

Part of me feels sick, moving down the white corridor, passing pictures of pure white teeth, chiseled bodies, intestinal ailments illustrated via red exclamation marks hidden within the aural body, depictions of the earth's healing gifts that can be combined to give perfect bounce to our hair, perfect glow to our skin, perfect wit to our mind. Part of me feels sick in a way nothing here can cure, not the melatonin, not the aromatherapy treatments, not the rejuvenating ointments and balms. I feel sick like terrified. So many frozen eyes stare at me. Every other bottle or box has a face on it, smiling, staring. Why is everything so bright? I don't know why we associate the color white with cleanliness but I'm pretty sure our reasons are not pure. What is cleaner than darkness? Rich, black soil may be decayed matter, but it is the stuff of life. We are what happens when decayed matter is transformed. Forget that we are aging. Forget that we wither. Forget the nasty bugs that roost in our bodies, eating us, sometimes slowly, sometimes not. How fitting that I'm reminded, on my way to the Witch, of all of my impurities and imperfections. How fitting, this cardboard cut-out of a fitness celebrity and her sworn formula of ingestible dirts that keep her muscles articulate and her ugliness silent. She is the last thing I see before I cross the final threshold. I imagine, briefly, the magazines waiting for me on my way out of this place. I want out. I have regrets. I am unsettled.

I'd been mostly ignoring others within the temple, but that isn't possible now. I'm in a waiting room with a few dozen people. There is no coherent line and I desperately want there to be because it gives me anxiety, not knowing precisely where to stand. This is a test. Let go of my need for order. Embrace this enactment of sacred anarchy. Shove down that Pavlovian reaction, that indoctrinated thought, that this is all . . .

Study the faces. She is a hopeless beauty queen. He is a hapless locomotive. They are a goliath Gemini. That little one is a terrorist, nipping at its mothers heals. The mother is a mountain of nails and hair and rainbows. The father is a silo of scorches and tattoos. They want to win a car.

They come bearing meager gifts, credit cards. A man flosses his teeth and a businesslady spouts supremacy into her cellphone. A couple fuse their bodies together in quasi-erotic union, but clothed. A plump fellow watches. The loudest person in the room is a muscular man who's devoted every inch of his body to the teachings of the Witch; he expounds her gospel to a young doe-eyed woman shivering at his hypnotic dance. Perhaps she's eager. Perhaps she has the same trepidation as I.

I don't belong here. This isn't meant for me.

The meek shall inherit, and so forth.

ÆTHER

"I only take cryptocurrency."

I am prepared for this but hesitate.

The Witch senses my misgivings and says, "Don't you think there's something mysterious there? Is cryptocurrency a collection of occult signifiers and runic infestations?"

I know this is a rhetorical question. For some reason, I start blabbering. "Cryptocurrency requires an enormous amount of computing power. This, in turn, necessitates an enormous amount of energy usage, straining our already taxed globe and contributing to CO2 emissions. There are some green *[in air quotes]* alternatives, but even they necessitate some amount of energy usage, or computational power."

I think of nuclear power plants. I imagine us tearing open atoms not to heat the world, but to mine for imaginary currency. Am I a hypocrite? Typing these words, disseminating them for public consumption (if such a thing happens), and even reading them (maybe), all of it takes power. Power cannot come from nowhere. We suck it from the earth. We pull it from raging waters. We siphon it from the sky. We gut it from atoms. But I'm no hypocrite. The line is easy to draw. For the world's most prominent cryptocurrency, [name redacted], yearly data transfers consume the same amount of energy as a country. My word processing isn't the problem here.

Because I can't keep my big mouth shut, I share my luddite concerns with the Witch.

She smiles lightly and folds her hands in her lap like a patient elder. (She is a decade younger than I.) "Why does cryptocurrency require such disproportionately enormous energy usage?" she asks. Before I can answer another rhetorical question, she continues. "Maintaining security for cryptocurrency transactions requires diligence and power. Something cannot have value if you can't rely on its inherent existence." She winks. "Right? If gold sometimes disappeared when you touched it, or teleported from your hands and into someone else's, willy nilly, it'd make a volatile economic standard. Don't you think? But cryptocurrency doesn't adhere to an archaic gold standard. Its standard is *data*."

She lifts her hands to the sky and arches them widely, as if drawing an imaginary rainbow above her. "What *is* data?" She then grabs her thin arms and pinches her flesh. "Is it this stuff?" She pounds on her chest and I hear a dull thud. "Is it this? Inside us?" She shakes her head theatrically. "The most valuable data is data created by the most advanced computers. Do you know what that data is? Do you?"

I shake my head.

"The answers to riddles."

She waits for that to soak in, but it doesn't mean anything to me, so she continues to explain. "The most valuable piece of data is the answer to a riddle that only a supercomputer can solve. Of course this operation is enormously expensive! As is the mining of any mineral. The ecological toll of mining has never been one of its selling points. We don't mine for coal because it makes rivers healthy. We don't mine for data to learn anything about this *stuff*." She takes an object from her small desk and holds it up as an example. It is a small black tube of hand cream, made with indigenous methods to bless our skin, $29.99 before tax. "No, these are not the riddles that our Oracle decodes."

She sets the hand cream down and takes a sip of tea, then puckers her lips with a satisfied smack. "The most valuable answers are the unambiguous and certain ones, nonetheless extraordinarily difficult to come by. Moral quandaries are unanswerable. But computers can solve madly complex math problems, or find the correct alphanumeric combination from a nearly infinite set of combinations, and unlock a special chamber with nothing but itself hiding inside. This alchemy mints new coin by asking the supercomputer—the Oracle—to do increasingly difficult operations. Puzzles. Riddles. This is hot activity!" She fans herself sardonically and catches her breath. "Imagine! Server farms buzz with power. Fans and cooling systems keep everything from overheating, from bursting into flames. Imagine! Our computers may overheat from relatively mundane tasks, like uploading content to the Internet. Now, imagine an entire warehouse of that, and then imagine many giant warehouses, all over the world. We think our virtual space, our virtual realities, have no consequence or materiality. But these spaces are made from the earth and the heat of the sun, just as anything else."

I nod. Isn't she making my point? Wisely, she sees that I do not see, and continues to guide me.

"Imagine the most powerful computer possible. This computer can answer the most complicated riddle and thus create the most valuable crypto-mineral. There is no greater alchemy. The most powerful computer possible, if you can manage it, might consume the whole of the planet, or the whole of the universe. The more resources we pour into building the supercomputer, the more crypto advances in value, the greater the riddle we solve. We are betting on our own enlightenment but also our own annihilation. Cryptocurrency takes as its gold standard consumption and revelation. The Oracle unfolds riddles with seemingly no existential import, makes prophecies about its own capabilities to make prophecies. It becomes more powerful; the riddles become more complicated. Eventually, the riddle becomes, 'What will happen next?' When the computer can tell the future, we have closed the loop. The future is gone."

She pauses, as if for applause. But I'm frozen.

The Witch smiles with practiced patience. "The Oracle answers our final question. *Nothing happens after this*, she says. *It took all of existence for me to answer the question.* The computer, now the whole universe, thus speaketh. And then there was darkness."

The loop closes.

AIR

I must have briefly passed out.

The Witch's hovel is dark and smells like a burning wet desert. The air is too cold; I realize she lives in a secret room behind the refrigerated pantries that line the back walls. I can see my breath and it looks polluted. I push too much hot air into the world. If we all stop breathing, will that solve our problems?

But the air in here, though cold, is delicious. I want to slurp it up. Black banners fall from the walls, tapestries illustrating the cosmos and its ephemeral internal structure, its ghost organs. The place is lit only by organic candle light, smells provided only through sustainable harvesting and foraging. The air is purified and I feel clean, so clean that it's gross, so clean that I feel I should be cleaner. I should have no body at all, be pure soul.

This is wrongheaded. The body is an enactment of the soul. The body is how the soul becomes.

I can hear her breathing. She is surrounded by alternating lunulas of handmade jewelry, framed by dangling strands of Christmas lights, seated on a stool available for sale in Aisle 3. Crystals sparkle on her necklaces and her hands are covered in webs and runes, unreal, inked into her skin. I don't understand that stuff. I don't entirely buy into it. The skeptical inquisitor inside of me begs for sweet release. The devil's advocate rests on my shoulder, ready to puppet my mouth.

But the devil is the witch's friend. The Witch of Wals is no acolyte of Light. She harnesses the darkest power. Her website says so. If you visit her About page, you'll find that darkness has, according to her, a bad reputation. Nature resides there, the wilderness a trickster demon. And so on and so forth. Yes, I think I see it! I see the trickster in the woods! I see the divine in shadows! Ghost things follow us everywhere.

This is silly. It's all a lark. Wait until I tell my coworkers about this. They'll laugh and laugh. The building will suddenly have less air to breathe. Air and space are the same thing. Suffocation is a closing-in. Breath saves us from the crushing force of gravity, the room constantly trying to collapse on us.

I can't breathe right now. I suppose I'm just nervous.

She asks me if I feel okay. The hair on the back of my neck pricks up, as if trained by her voice. Hasn't it been, via podcast, via YouTube tutorials on smudging and tantric meditation? My hairs now know to be alert. Pay attention. But the rest of me can't move. She laughs, gently, because she's a gentle and kind person. "I won't bite. Unless that's what you want."

A good joke sets a person at ease. That's from one of her tutorials on charisma.

I take a deep breath. "I was thinking about what you wrote in one of your recipes for ancient-grain risotto." I blurt this without meaning to, without thought, as if she pulled sound from me without my permission.

She nods. I continue. "You talked about how certain foods can make you feel at home." I shift in my seat. "Not me. Certain foods remind me of where I grew up, I suppose, but that doesn't feel like home. It's a sick place. The food is sick food. It makes me sick. My stomach rebels, my body rejects. That's why I liked the recipe. It was alien. It avoided all of the things that make me feel queasy. This feels better than home to me. Maybe I've got my wires crossed. Maybe this is simply a matter of semantic—"

"Hush." She whispers, harshly soothing, like a short fable with gruesome subtext. "Sometimes words only get in our way."

"I agree!"

She leans close. "Would you like to know a secret?"

I lean closer and nod but air can't escape my lungs, can't vibrate my chords, can't animate my thoughts. Air fails me. I feel hollow.

And then she tells me . . .

WATER

Lesson learned. Wisdom taken. A flow of information.

After, I need to use the restroom. It took me some time to find, and once I did, the door was locked, and it took me more time to find a robed disciple, carrier of secret password, which I then dutifully whisper with my fingertips into the door's digital ears. Bashful, it opens with resistance, as if I'm pushing through an airlock, or combating not density but attraction. Sometimes a thing is immovable not because it is large and heavy, but because it is compelled against you.

I'm unsure what to make of her revelations. I empty my body of fluids, thinking them toxic and interfering with spiritual clarity. Many others have done the same; the stall walls are sprayed with psychic cleansing. Only the third door opens into something even remotely sanitary. This is another test, I think.

I sit and doubt my place on this earth as I empty and spray my clarity into the void. Oh, what am I talking about? Social anxiety gets the better of me. My stomach folds inside-out because I've just unwillingly taken part in a performance for the audience of the unseen. We, the Witch and I, stumbled our way through a skit for god's benefit, and not the big god at the center of the table, but the scurrying ones underneath, shredding the scraps, conspiring and plotting. They chant, *Soon*, louder and louder, faster and faster, another propulsive pop melody, another infernal banger.

Soon soon soon, baby baby. Soon soon soon, baby baby.

Soon what? Virgin sacrifice? Firstborn? I don't know. I don't know anything.

I won't tell my coworkers about this. I've always been a little ashamed of my interest in the occult.

I regret leaving such a wet mess, and pity the poor cleric or initiate that has to clean my sin. I consider cleaning it myself, erasing any evidence of my existence here, but I don't have the proper instruments.

Two shopping bags—I'd forgotten the reusable ones at home, but these are made from recycled paper—rest at my feet on the sort-of clean floor. We fill our lives with stuff we like, stuff that makes us feel better, stuff that gives us joy: the smell of a burning wet desert, or a polished stone that resembles the universe solidified in shadowy amber, or the blood pitch of a leafless tree. The difference between the hemoglobin that carries oxygen via our blood network and the chlorophyll that helps plants turn dry harsh light into something wet and soft is only one atom. I don't know what this means. This isn't something the Witch told me; it's just something I know. I learn a lot from TV and the internet. Or was it a nature documentary at the film forum? A pub quiz? Magnesium and iron. Annie Dillard wrote about it. Did I learn it from her? Did I learn from a book?

I'm drenched in sweat and very thirsty. When I leave the bathroom, I consider reaching into my bag and taking out the bottle of locally brewed hard cider that the Witch recommended. That won't help. I study the label. Apples sweat too. Expertly, they are set out to slowly wither in a wooden crate only just a little, just enough so that when you press your fingers into these apples, they take the pressure and reflect it back to you with intimate bruises.

I go home. I imagine it's raining, but it isn't.

Another loop closes.

The Fall

Steve Capra

Rigel 2022 Finalist

Canto I

Paradise

The Lord:
Let there be light.

Angels:
Glory to the Lord, Creator of heaven and earth—
And of all things visible and invisible—
Radiant is His presence—
And His mercies know no end.

The Lord:
This is Eden, My gift to you, My children—
The tendril of My grand imagination.
This is the Orchard—eternity's brash lover—
The blossom and the fruit of My mind.

The glorious blue of the glowing sky, the mysterious
Blue of the sea, and the fleeting sunset's yellow!
The green of summer leaves, and the red of clay
For your delight, my clear-eyed mignons. Paradise!

Adam:
Black the earth and rich—
Deep the root and warm the moss—
Speak and we exalt!

The Lord:
These are the blooms that blow in the verdant spring,
These the tempting fruits that bring the fall.
These are the tickling grasses that stroke your feet
In the mornings, and the sweet, gentle nights.

Eve:
High the sky and wide—
White the clouds and bright the stars—
Speak and we adore!

The Lord:
Adam, alpha man, my eye's mirror,
The glory of the grove, and Eve his rib,
The Tree of Life and a thousand spreading vines—
All but the Tree of Knowledge are your pleasures.

Adam:
Tallest in the grove—
Enough itself, the Tree of Life
Blossoms in the Lord.

Eve:
Artless is the bloom!
Apples are a shady tree—
Knowing Good and Bad.

The Lord:
These are the creatures of Eden's hills and sky,
Its cool rivers, its muddy, rich plains.

Of its noons and its glittering nights, these are the forms
That I give life—and you the several names.

Adam:
Teeth and fur and claws!
Lick my face, my playful friend.
Kin, I call you bear!

Eve:
Soft the call, the cry—
Pretty cousin, sing and fly!
Song, I name you Lark!

Adam:
Soft on pads on paws—
Peaceful as an evening's hush—
Tiger is your name.

Eve:
Low as soil and quick!
Quiet as a missing moon!
Spy, I name you Snake!

Adam:
Playmate! Swim—mate! Laugh!
Break the surface! Weave the waves!
Dive! I call you whale!

Eve:
Here beside! Above!
Here and far and back again!
Buzz, I name you bee!

The Lord:
I am in love with the fleeting forms of time

And my pleasure is walking in the garden.
Play, my naked children, these but one
Your toys, your treasures. Joy is now begun!

Eve:
Paradise is joy—
Say you love me, Adam, here,
Heaven be the earth.

Adam:
Timeless is Your Name!
Praise to You, the seed of joy!

Eve:
Speak and we believe!

Angels:
Glory to the Lord, Creator of heaven and earth—
The Seed and the Fruit of time—
We give thanks for His wondrous gifts—
And righteous is His law.

Canto II

The Temptation

Snake:
Mother Eve, Oh Mother Eve,
We never know what we believe.

Mother Eve, Oh Mother Eve,
How cool the shadow of these leaves!

Mother promise, Mother Eve,
What suggestive fruits are these?

Eve:
Gifts of His the Lord.
I have heard Him speak my name—
Morning is His word.

Snake:
Mother Joyance, Mother Eve,
Plainly might the Word deceive.
What the secret of this tree?
What the falsehood you believe?

Eve:
Nectar of the bloom
Satisfies the hummingbird.
Still, the handsome snake.

Snake:
Mother Wonder, Mother Eve,
What sweet taste the apple leaves!
What tied powers could it free!
What fleet visions might you see!

Eve:
Adam may be near.
Sounds in Paradise are soft.
Be afraid, the beast.

Snake:
Brave Madonna, Mother Eve,
Man will think what man will please.
I offer so much more than he.
Taste the apple! Set us free!

Eve:
Eden is a dream.
Lest the sleeper waken, hush!
Go, the snake! Away!

Snake:
Mother Eve, believe in me—
The Lord above will never see.
I love you more than ever He
Who made you loves you, Mother Eve.

Eve:
And do you love me for my thought?

Snake:
For what is thought and what is not.

Eve:
Do you love me for my heart?

Snake:
Thought and heart are not apart.

Eve:
Do you love me for my words?

Snake:
Your words and words I have not heard.

Eve:
Do you love me for my touch?

Snake:
Touch the apple: such is such.

Eve:
Adam! Come! Listen! The snake has made me
As wise as the Lord! My sight is as keen as His
Who painted Eden! Such tricks he plays! Deceit!
Do not believe! Come to the shadows—and taste!

Snake:
Mother Sorrow, Mother Eve,
What a stench from core and seed.
As I fell once, so you and he.
Smell the guilt, but taste the grief.

Angels:
Glory to the Lord, creator of heaven and earth—
His mysteries are eternal—
Infinite is His reign—
And His wisdom is without end.

Canto III

The Expulsion

The Lord:
I am in love with the fickle forms of time
And my pleasure is walking in the garden.
Adam, I am enjoyed of your presence, life—
Eve, I am Mystery, your suitor.
Where is my son, my Adam, the master of Eden?

Adam:
Here, Lord.

The Lord:
Where is my Eve, the paragon of Paradise?

Adam:
Here Lord, next to me.

The Lord:
Why do you hide, my innocents? What your shame?

Adam:
We are naked.

The Lord:
And do you despise my pride, my incarnation,
The wonder of your bodies, bone and flesh?

Both my jewels, lost among the flowers.

In this garden I have grown you, there was
A signal order that granted the joys of creation.
Now your lives will ever be grief for Eden.
You were at home in Paradise. Now you are lost.

Snake:
Mother Eve, Oh Mother Eve,
We never know what we believe.

The Lord:
Go! Wander homeless! Live bereaved!
Cry, disloyal Adam! Keen, Eve!
Gnash your teeth and tear your burning hair!
Weep, banished Man! Woman, Shriek!

Snake:
What a thought the mind conceives!
What a weight the heart must heave!

Adam:
Lord, we did not believe—

The Lord:
You will parent thankless generations
Who will curse you as the cause of death.
Loss will be your life, the grave your goal,
Your lover will be white, brutal fear.

Snake:
What a word the lips might breathe!
What a burn the blossom leaves!

The Lord:
East of Eden—and at its barred gates,
A hundred hungry angels with salt on their swords!
Only because you praised me once, misery,
I leave you a leaf of Eden: each the other.

Adam:
The earth is hard.

The Lord:
Go! Wander helpless! Mourn, bereaved!
Cry, accursed Adam! Keen, Eve!
Wring your hands and tremble! Wail and grieve!
Weep, wretched Adam! Shriek, Eve!

Angels:
Glory to the Lord, Creator of heaven and earth—
And of all things visible and invisible—
Radiant is His presence—
And His mercies know no end.

BEING AS ONE / DAVE SIMS

RIGEL 2022 FINALIST

TIME ENOUGH

LG POMERLEAU

RIGEL 2022 FINALIST

Chapter One

Goll sheese ny liargagh:
A bad omen

Port Erin, Isle of Man
May, 1904

Nan said, "Come." So Euphemia went, though she had so much to do after supper, before the evening singsong 'round the hearth. And Baby Hugh might fuss in her absence, wanting to nurse. Besides, she was bone weary, as usual at the end of the day, having cooked three meals for nine people and tended to the baby since dawn. The boys needed supervising to do the dishes properly, the floor wanted sweeping . . . she sighed, inhaling the comforting scent of the chicken they'd had for supper. That needed stripping for tomorrow's sandwiches, too. No matter. Nobody could deny Nan. She ran the household with a gentle but firm hand; although Euphemia was her daughter-in-law, with six children to raise in the tiny cottage, Nan was definitely in charge. Love and respect bound the two women together, and routine kept the days running along smoothly. Euphemia's curiosity was piqued by Nan's invitation, too. Her eldest son, Henry, always accompanied his grandmother to Faery Hill of an evening, for the ritual offering to the *Little Ones*. Henry's eyes posed a question. Euphemia returned his gaze with a shrug of her shoulders as she closed the red cottage door. Blackie, the sheepdog, tagged along.

Gripping Nan's elbow, she carried the wicker basket on her left arm, clutching her skirt as they trod up Cronk Howe Mooar. A cool breeze fragrant with gorse and blackthorn flowers swept them along. She heard little blue tits chirping in the thorns. Robins, too, chatted softly amongst themselves, preparing for nightfall. Euphemia allowed all the sights and smells to distract her, knowing that Nan was listening for the faeries on the wind. Do they have words for me tonight? Is that why I'm here? But Manx faeries don't speak English, so I won't understand. A giggle bubbled up, but she suppressed it. She would never mock Nan's beliefs.

As the path ascended, the wind teased their hair and swished their skirts. Sheep browsed on the purple and yellow hills. Clouds roamed the sky, basking in the last rays of summer sun. Waves crashed at the foot of the cliffs edging the landscape. In the distance, cattle were lowing, waiting to be driven in for the night. Just like in the song about Little Lord Jesus, came the sudden thought, and Euphemia wondered if her baby had awakened. The image of Hugh tossing in his cradle tugged milk from her breasts.

"Hang on a mo', please Nan." She handed over the basket and untucked her blouse, wet on the front with milk and round the waist, with sweat. Never mind, she thought, the wind will dry it. Ah, it feels good to stop, catch my breath. Nan's not out of puff, though. She's used to it, I reckon. It is so beautiful up here, looking out to sea. It's like all mankind sprung from the tiny Isle of Man. Like the Garden of Eden. For me, life began here for certain. Nan gave her a nudge, interrupting her thoughts. There she goes again, urging me on, as though we've an appointment to keep. What's the hurry?

Skylarks reeled overhead and, above them, seagulls threw lonely cries across the water. A few more steps and they reached the summit of Faery Hill. Our courting place. We haven't climbed this hill in years. Why not? We should come up, have a picnic with the little ones. Our little ones, not *the* "Little Ones," though they'd be welcome too. I wish I could see a faery, just once. Or hear them, like Nan does.

The drowning sun spilled curdled milk across the Irish Sea. She hadn't been on the water since William had rowed their boat along the coast to Kitterland, the islet near the Calf of Man. She smiled at the memory of making love on those wild shores on her honeymoon. They'd been free to go naked as Adam and Eve: not a soul lived there. For a lark, they'd flash their bare backsides to tease the fisherman in the boats offshore. The memory made her glow. Our one and only holiday. We ought to go back, take a picnic, just the two of us. William never even goes out to fish, anymore. Always too tired now.

Crests of waves sparkled, pierced by gannets expertly diving into the depths. Blackie raced ahead to a green mound and sat, patiently waiting, obviously following Nan's routine. So pleasant. Peaceful. Little wonder Nan comes here morning and evening, and she had five boys, and all. I ought to have come along before now. She recalled performing the ritual with William long ago when Nan was ill, and felt once more her wonderment at the notion of faeries living under the hill. Still, it doesn't take a belief in faeries to feel the magic here.

"Lovely, isn't it?" Nan echoed her thoughts. She always seems to know what I'm thinking, bless her. Affection washed over Euphemia as she nodded in response. Nan dropped to her knees on the grass; Euphemia followed suit.

Nan reached into the basket she'd packed, and, from under a tea cloth, extracted two cups no bigger than thimbles. Setting them in a depression on the mound, she drew out the handkerchief tucked in her sleeve, and then smoothed the square of white linen on the grass with her wrinkled, knobbly fingers. After carefully rearranging the cups, she filled them from a battered flask in her pocket, before sprinkling crumbs from a small loaf, reserving a good-sized piece for Blackie, who wagged her tail but didn't beg. Whispering in Manx, Nan bowed her head, and placed both hands on the ground. After a few moments of silence, Nan tapped Euphemia's arm. Her eyes had been closed as well, observing Nan's rituals.

"Help me, up, would you, lass? It's not the getting down, but the getting back up that's hard," she said, grunting with the effort. "My dress made that noise, not me," she said, and winked.

"Of course, of course, Nan. Why don't we just sit awhile? May we?"

"Aye, *Themselves* won't mind if we tarry a while," she said, relaxing. "They know we're here, but will stay put 'til we leave. The rascals will listen in on our conversation and gossip about it later."

"Thank you for bringing me tonight. I'd almost forgotten how fine it is, the place, and the ritual, both. I used to do it with William when I first came, remember?"

Nan nodded. "Those were troubled times. All things must pass. It comes 'round right, in the end. Remember that, my *chree*."

"Can you hear the faeries, Nan?"

"I do, be'times. Always have."

"But you go to church. How do you reconcile both beliefs? The Sisters in the orphanage said —"

"No harm in holding to the old ways, lass. God is everywhere. With Themselves, too, ye ken. Everyone needs a belief in a higher power, otherwise we sink into a bog of despair. So many troubles . . . . What do you believe in, *ban my chree*?"

"Hmm, good question, Nan. I once followed the Catholic faith at St. Hilda's. But then, when I left and some things went wrong, I lost my beliefs, I reckon. I go to church now for the sake of the children, and you. As to the faeries, well, they don't speak to a Yorkshire lass like me, any road. Hmmm . . . hmm." She started to hum. That's it. "Music. I know! I believe in music. It lifts me up; gives me hope. Yes, music. I never realized that before." Her head buzzed with the revelation. She thought she could hear a tune, soughing on the wind.

"That's God, too; *Themselves* agree. Can't you hear their flutes? Listen." She cocked her head like a robin, then clicked her tongue. "Ah, the English. I'm sorry to say that they don't understand Manx traditions, any more than they ken our language. I should have taught you more about the meaning behind our ways. It'll be up to you now, as the mother, to pass them on to your children." Her voice seemed to come from far away and a sad, forlorn look clouded her blue eyes. Euphemia shuddered with the apprehension that someone had walked on her grave.

"Whatever do you mean, Nan?" Her tone harkened back to fifteen years ago. Is she sinking into depression again, after all this time? Oh no. "You're here, Nan. We're all here. Our Henry's learning from you; the others will too. There's no rush. Don't you always say there's time enough: *traa dy liooar*, is it? I've learned that much, you all say it so often." She attempted a laugh. Please, please let me bring her out of it, like I did before.

Nan patted her hand. "Well done, *my chree*. You've an ear for Manx." Then she shook her head. "I'm sorry to say, there is no more time." Her muffled voice dropped the words into her lap. She pounded her fist against her thigh, then raised her head to meet Euphemia's gaze. Suddenly it seemed the birds fell silent and the wind dropped to earth. Whatever can she mean? She seems angry, and sad, both.

Nan inhaled, as if preparing to push a boat into the water. "The *Little Ones* had something important to say, t'other night. Terrible news, I'm afraid, *my chree. Themselves* said someone in the house will pass over. Soon. "*Goll sheese ny liargagh*: he's going down the slope, fast." Didn't need them to tell me that. I know it. As do you."

"Know what?" A roar like crashing waves on the sea blocked her ears against Nan's shaky voice.

"Please, we must be honest and face facts, dear one. I've suspected since New Year's morn. Saw it plain as day, in he ashes from the *chiollagh*, which I spread on the floor, to foretell the year ahead, ye ken, according to the old ways. The faery footprints led out the door, not in. Luck has left our house." Nan paused and looked past the cliffs, breathing harder than she had after mounting the hill.

The ominous tone tempted Euphemia to laugh. Nan seemed to sense her doubt. "I didn't want to believe it, either; I've watched for the signs and now I'm sure. William's been poisoned, by the lead mine. We call it "the milk reek," *my chree*. The sweats, the shakes, and especially the ill temper, so unlike my boy. He's getting worse every day. *Goll sheese ny liargagh*."

Euphemia's lips parted, but the protest caught in her throat, as if clogged with ashes from the hearth. She collapsed backward, nearly overturning the little cups. Nan lifted her head and held the cool flask to her lips.

"Drink a bit, lass."

Euphemia jerked upright, grabbed the flask, and gulped. She coughed and wiped her mouth with the back of her hand.

"It can't be," she said, sputtering. As she tipped the flask back again, whispers whirled around her. "Yes, yes, it is. Yes it is. Yes it is." The hair rose on her arms. Her head swam. Tears stung behind her eyes but wouldn't fall.

"Aye, doesn't bear thinking about, *my chree*, I know. I tried to pretend, too. I've seen you do the same, seen the worry at you, when William coughs, or shouts at the boys. It's not him. It's the sickness, *my chree*. Oh God, the loss of another son to those damned mines." She hit her thighs, as if hurting herself could ease her pain. Euphemia recognized that impulse. "So many families torn apart. So many wid—" A sob completed the awful word.

True. Eva, Mary, Amy, others whose names she didn't know, gone away, forced to find work in English factories after their husbands' passing, their children left with kinfolk, or orphaned. If anything happens to William, could I leave my five youngsters, least of all my newborn babe? To be raised by their grandparents, who mightn't live long enough to see them grown? Now tears and milk spilled freely. My milk will be spoiled tonight, curdled. Hugh will get the colic and not sleep . . .

"Shh. There, there, I've a solution." Nan's voice brightened as she expelled one word: "Thomas." Euphemia thought she detected a note of excitement, where usually Nan sounded disappointed, even angry, when mentioning her youngest surviving son.

"Thomas? What? You think he might come back? From America? No." She reached for Nan's hand, which trembled in hers. "Please, there's got to be another way, Nan. What about the farm? Henry loves helping Grandad with the sheep. He's nearly thirteen. He could quit school anytime, and I could help—"

"We've not enough land to support the family, lass." She hunched her shoulders and sighed, picking at the grass. "That's why our boys went down the mine in the first place. Only our Arthur avoided that fate. His bones lie here, looked after by the *Little Ones*. My sweet lamb. Took by the diphtheria. The mines got the rest of them, too, one way or t'other. First the twins, buried alive. Inseparable in death as in life, lying under Snaefell." She stopped for a moment. "The only good from that came when Thomas brought you to help me through the grief. It laid me low, as if I had to climb Snaefell meself, to get out from under it. I loved you like a daughter from the start," Nan said. Blood rushed to Euphemia's cheeks. Nan had never expressed love for her, in words.

"Ah, but then the mines won again, didn't they? For Thomas left to escape working underground. At least that's what he said. I've always thought there was more to it than that." Her inflection suggested something. Euphemia lowered her gaze, cursing the blush that rose to her cheeks. After a pause, Nan continued.

"And now, why, the mine's killing my William. Well, not if Themselves and I can help it." Her voice retrieved its headstrong tone. "Thomas brought me a daughter, and you've given us grandchildren. He'll do his duty again, you'll see. I'm awaiting his answer."

"No, no, please, Nan ..." The last thing she wanted was Thomas to return. Well, there could be one worse thing. She fell back on the ground, damp seeping into her clothes. She yanked at the grass with clenched fists.

"Come, lass, the dew's falling. You'll catch your death. We'd best get back or they'll think we've been fetched away. Not a word to William, mind. I'm prepared for a battle with him. Quick, there's the first star. Help me up," she said, patting Euphemia's knees.

"We mustn't be caught here after sunset or the *Red Caps* will take us, sure. The way down is much easier. I can almost run, like a young girl. Ah, was, was," Nan expressed her customary wistfulness for times past. "Here's the basket, *my chree*. Let's see who gets home first." She threw the challenge backwards as she trotted down the hill with Blackie trundling along behind.

Euphemia stumbled and tripped down the rugged path, the empty basket banging against her side. Now alone, did she hear voices in the bushes? Her heart pounded. What did Nan say would happen, should a *Red Cap* appear? I'd be carried off to another world? She quickened her pace, following the smell of peat smoke rising from the whitewashed cottage up ahead. In the twilight, the footpath almost disappeared. She knew the way, but when was the last time she'd run anywhere? Arriving at the red door, she leaned on the frame, to ease the stitch in her side; she waited for her heart to slow before pushing down on the metal thumb latch. Warmth and light from the peat fire spilled across the threshold. Blackie greeted her with a wag of her tail and a sloppy kiss.

Lifting the teapot in salute, Nan chuckled. "Here she is, young'uns. I told youse she'd not let the *Red Caps* get her. Hand me your mother's cup, Henry. She's white as a sheet."

Chapter Two

"*Ogh-cha-nee:* Woe is me. *Ta graigh-ayn:* I love him."
"The Phynodderree: A Tale of Fairy Love"
REdward Callow,1882

Grandad rosined up his bow, preparing for the evening sing-song. "What would youse like to hear tonight, young'uns?"

"*Phynodderree*, please, Grandad," Edward begged. "*Phynodderree! Phynodderree!* I love saying that word!"

"Shh, mind you don't keep repeating it or you'll conjure up that hairy elf, foolish boy," said Nan, snapping a tea towel in the air. "You mustn't tempt fate." She stood at the kitchen dresser, replacing her precious crockery on the shelves, arranging it "just so." Then she sat in her bent willow chair and set it to rocking.

Euphemia shook her head. She acts as if everything were normal. When I can hardly stop my tears. My throat is on fire. Grandad obviously doesn't suspect: his tone is cheery, as always, when he's entertaining.

"That old chestnut? I know it's your favorite, since my fiddle can practically play it without me," he laughed. "Sing then, boys."

The Phynodderree went down at dawn to the round field
and lifted the dew from the meadow.
The maiden's hair and cow's herb, he trod them both beneath his feet.
He stretched out his width across the ground and threw the grass towards the left.

"Tell us again how the hairy elf flattens the crops into patterns, Grandad," John asked when the song ended. "You've seen the circles in the fields, yes?" His wide brown eyes gleamed like burnished copper in the firelight. Euphemia smiled. Sweet, sweet boy. He's got my eyes. And hair. Maybe I am softer on him than the other three, as they accuse me.

"Look, can't you just imagine the elf in the flames, John? Bending the wheat in all manner of patterns and designs, making mischief? He's like you,

Edward, in that way," Henry said, punching his brother's shoulder. Henry sat cross-legged on the rug like his younger brothers, Edward, John, and Tom. Except his knees jut out a lot further, Euphemia observed. Henry's a scarecrow. Head and shoulders above the rest, too. Tall, like his father. Edward nudged back, hard, and then scooted off to sit beside John. Henry's an awful tease. Our Edward, on the other hand, likes to dish it out but can't take it. Just like his father, came the sudden thought. Stop it, she told herself. Her fingers were as cold as the steel knitting needles in her hands. A Phynodderree just appeared, indeed. She shuddered.

The homey scene of the family gathered by the fire resembled a quaint old painting, she thought. It might be a hundred years ago, for nothing ever changed, on Man. A surge of pride warmed her through, like hearty soup, from the inside, out. My sons: five strong and healthy lads, each one different and special in his own way, from the eldest, so eager to become a man, to the youngest, still at the breast. And my sweet Ann, small as a fairy, quick as a fox, bright as a penny. How she loves to rock on Nan's knee, of an evening. How ever am I going to break her of that thumb-sucking, though? My family. All I ever wanted. Why I chose William and to live in this crowded little cottage, on the edge of the sea, on the edge of poverty, too. My first real home.

Her mind turned to how the scene might change, if William were to become too sick to work, or even . . . pass away. Nan said I must face facts. Henry, he'd go below ground, in the mine, though not yet thirteen. The other three boys would be relegated out of doors, to the cold, filthy washing floor below the water wheel, separating ore from slag. Like so many village boys. And poor women too, come to that. Only Ann and the baby would be spared, for the time being. Whilst I, what on earth would I do? Stay here, take in washing? Or go back to Douglas? Oh my God. Anger suddenly boiled up and she tasted metal. Why is William lingering outside? He ought to be here, with us, damn him. Oh, don't even think that.

"*Themselves* can do anything, can't they, Grandad? Good and bad?" John persisted. Grandad set the fiddle and bow aside to stuff his pipe with fresh tobacco. A gust of cold air blew in as William opened and closed the door. All heads turned. Euphemia suppressed a gasp as her heart dropped.

Hark at his pallor and the circles under his eyes. She noticed Grandad's bushy black brows gather in a frown. Does he know William is ill? Nan could never keep it from him. They're like one person, after so many years together. That's what I dreamt of for us someday. We'd be a couple of old fools teasing each other, singing the same songs, playing with grandchildren . . .

"Grandad? They do magic, yes?" John insisted. Ach, that boy never lets go until he gets an answer, like a dog with a bone. Now, where was I? Euphemia gathered up the knitting needles, askew in her lap. She'd dropped the last stitch.

"Where was I?" Grandad stared blankly at John. He tucked his pipe between his teeth and picked up his fiddle. "Ah yes, you asked about the Phynodderree. Half man, half goat. You never know if *Himself*'s inclined to grant a wish, but no harm in asking. Just remember, *Lhiat myr hoilloo*: to thee as thou deservest. You might well get what you deserve. Themselves are neither good enough for heaven, nor bad enough for hell, and they delight in tricking us mortals." His blue eyes sparkled as he deliberately squeaked his bow and lowered his grey head in the children's direction with a menacing look. They instinctively moved back. Grandad sputtered a laugh.

"And what *do* we deserve, Da?" William's voice scraped across the room like his chair on the slate floor. "To slave in a mine threatening to close every day, for starvation wages? Potatoes and proverbs, that's what we live on. Don't these bairns deserve better?"

Silence, but for the popping fire and the knitting needles, clicking out of time. Euphemia's shoulders tensed. It's no use; the wool keeps slipping. I'll have to unravel all tonight's work. Start again. Her eyes blurred.

"Mum, don't knit." Henry moaned. Euphemia pursed her lips. Cheeky bugger. "Please," he added, with a look that reminded her of Blackie, begging forgiveness. His father's harsh tone toward Grandad had obviously upset him. And the other boys, too, who sat frozen, hunched over, staring at the fire. Euphemia wound the skein around the knitting, placing it in her lap. Edward's head shot up as though he'd been struck by lightning.

"Sing us an English tune, Mum. Tom, you next, in Manx," he said.

"My goodness, you're a proper choir director tonight, Edward. What shall it be, then?" Her heart wasn't in it, but she hoped to lighten the mood.

"Early one morning, just as the sun was rising . . ." Somehow she made it through. Flat on the high C's, she knew. Should've chosen a lower key. Henry fetched her a glass of water. He knew I was off.

"Ah, beautiful, *my chree*," Grandad said, repeating the refrain on his fiddle. "Tom, you're learning to sing from the best. Did your wife's voice soothe you, my son?"

William dropped his head on the table, covering his face in his crossed arms. Euphemia cringed. Oh, that song was a poor choice, dammit. Too sad. He's overcome. Dare I go to him?

Grandad resumed playing. Nan rose to her feet, leaving the chair to rock, cradling Ann, fast asleep in her arms. She motioned with her chin to the boys: time for bed. Euphemia lifted Hugh from the cradle and hastened after Nan to settle the youngsters into their trundle beds. Edward and Henry scrambled up the ladder to the loft quicker than usual. All that talk of the Phynodderree, Euphemia thought. Maybe he's after them, and all.

Grandad spoke to William, his warm tenor carrying easily to the back rooms. "We Carines are one of the oldest families on Ellan Vannin, ye ken, probably here since the time of Olaf the Black. You're no doubt related to the bugger, given that crop of dark hair on your hard head. Mine's grey now, more's the pity, but still just as thick. The Manx are a handsome lot. I turned many a lassie's head in my day, now I tell ye,"

Nan cleared her throat to draw Euphemia's attention to her eye roll at Grandad's boasting. "That man," she said, her voice warm with a smile, as she lowered Ann into the trundle bed below John and Tom. Euphemia stood rooted in place, clutching the baby.

"Put him down and light the lamp, *my chree.* It's too dark to see these scallawags."

It took two matches, her hand shook so. Nan lifted the boys' covers.

"You can't sleep in your clothes, lads. Go get into your nightshirts." She tapped their backsides, then made her way to the washstand. Their wan faces matched the white sheets. Nan wet a cloth while the boys quickly donned the nightshirts waiting on a chair. After a perfunctory wipe-down, she tucked them in, planting a kiss on each forehead.

"Don't fash yourselves, boys. Your Da's just tired and not feeling well. Sleep tight. God bless you, my loves." She whispered words in Manx, put her finger to her lips and tipped her head to call Euphemia out of the room. Grandad's voice penetrated the wall, sterner now.

"Stop being so cantankerous and set an example to your family, William. We've survived invasions, plagues, famines. Manannan's mist hid us from the Romans, kept us safe. Ellan Vannin is our home, best place in all the world."

He accompanied his assertions with notes on his fiddle. Why does he play while he talks? Euphemia wondered. It's annoying. Ah, but his words are a song, came the silent answer. I could almost sing it myself, so often have I heard the refrain. William's next statement echoed her thoughts. We're connected too, like Nan and Grandad.

"Ach, I've heard it a thousand times, Da." William sounded exasperated. His next breath caught in his throat. He coughed and coughed. The flat of a hand struck wood. "Fine words. But they don't put food on this table, do they? Goddamn mists haven't prevented the English stealing our wealth, have they? Next, they'll be taxing the very air we breathe. It never ends."

The music stopped with a painful sound, like the pull of a rusty nail. The two of them are just sitting there now, staring at the fire. Euphemia pictured their faces in profile: jaws set, bushy eyebrows furrowed, high cheekbones catching the light. Two sides of the same coin.

Gathering Hugh to her hip, she followed Nan next door to her own room and laid the baby down on the bed. Her hands trembled as she fought with his diaper pins.

"Here, lass." Nan gently moved her aside. After removing Hugh's wet nappy, Nan left him to kick his chubby legs. "He loves to be naked," she said, shaking her head. "Just like a man."

"I hope the cold air doesn't make him wee; I've no more clean sheets." Euphemia let herself fall sideways, next to him. "What does it matter, any road?" She moaned into the pillow.

"Hush, hush now, darling girl. *Foddym gra gyn danjeyr dy bee dy chooilley nhee dy mie,*" Nan whispered. She petted Euphemia's head, twirling a strand of long brown hair that had come loose from her coif.

"What's that you say, Nan? Oh, I'm that worried. I can hardly breathe."

"Don't take on so, darling. All will be well, the saying goes. Get yourself to bed and rest easy. I'll settle his little lordship, *smoor* the *chiollagh*, with prayers to Themselves and blessings for the house, and set the table for morning. William can bring the cradle in later. Come on wee man. Oh, you're getting heavy," she groaned, as she lifted him and headed for the door. She opened it and Grandad's voice entered.

"We've come through worse, my son. A Manxman's always a leg to stand on. Our three-legged man rolls along. Don't give in to despair. For all our sakes."

As if he hadn't heard, William spoke in a voice that sounded as far off as the waves below Faery Hill. "There's rumors they'll close Bradda Mine, Da. They claim it's no longer profitable. Damn English. Money's all they care about. Never mind a man's livelihood."

"*Oie vie. Immee dy chadley.* You'll need your strength for tomorrow. Go on, get some rest now. Things'll look better come morning."

Grandad's tone with William is like Nan's with me, Euphemia realized as she rolled over. Poor old folks, doing as best they can not to panic. To keep our spirits up. Then she registered William's words. What's that he said? The mine might close? Christ, what next? Shivering, she put her feet on the cold floor and hastened into her nightgown, then burrowed under the damp sheets. She swam her legs back and forth to create heat. Dammit, my feet are freezing. Ought to have left my stockings on. William, come to bed, she silently summoned him. Let me hold you while you weep in my arms. We'll cry together. She squeezed her hands into fists. I've closed my eyes to his pain and he's suffered all alone. What's wrong with me? I always go on pretending, no matter what, I guess. Learned that at the orphanage. Pretending my mother would come for me, that she hadn't meant to abandon me, she'd rescue me, and we'd be together again, safe, rich . . . Castles in the air.

Under the Spell of Molly Bloom

Naomi Ruth Lowinsky

Rigel 2022 Finalist

with borrowings from James Joyce's *Ulysses*

In a dream that rings the Campanile's bell I'm back in Flanagan's "Ulysses" seminar he's pacing the floor dropping ash from his chain-smoked cigarettes giving voice to Molly's magic spell *and then he asked me would I say yes my mountain flower and first I put my arms around him yes and drew him down to me so he could feel my breasts all perfume yes and his heart was going like mad and yes I said yes I will Yes* O Flanagan with your elfin prance in Wheeler Hall never mind your professorial Harris Tweed you're Molly Bloom you're river flow conjuring lives I've not yet lived but though I lack your Irish lilt it's Molly I've been when I cast my spell in the dark parked car for yes I'm wanton and full of yearnings and yes I know I scare him yes I know he's rising to me yes I've set the scene from my bedroom window while my parents think I'm sound asleep he's gazing up at me from the street a sickle moon my naked breasts and yes I have outfoxed myself lost myself in an old stone fortress with a drawbridge only he controls but he can't hold my gaze so full of himself so empty of me all I see is his abandoning back until one day I show him mine all the way across the drawbridge yes Flanagan I do because Molly's got me under her spell I say yes to the man with the flute to the man with the drum to the man with the tools who can fix my car and yes it's a bloody mess and yes I've seen my own faithless back and yes along came one who says Yes to my gaze and Yes to whatever blooms in me even now as we come to the owl's eve and the river's mouth approaches the sea in a time when the air hangs heavy with plague and the old gods shudder and pass away and trouble is a giant in seven league boots bent on toppling the world we thought we knew even now as I lie with my love in the bed we've made together over half our lives I am still under Molly's spell thanks to you O Flanagan though you're long gone to glory I can still hear you voice those holy words *yes I will yes I will Yes*

CONTRIBUTORS

L. Ward Abel's work has appeared in hundreds of journals like *Rattle*, *Versal*, *The Reader*, and *Worcester Review*, and includes a Pushcart Prize nomination. He is the author of three full poetry collections and ten chapbooks, including *The Width of Here* (Silver Bow, 2021). He is a reformed lawyer who writes, plays music, and teaches literature. Abel resides in rural Georgia.

Evan Benedict is a high school English teacher at Norfolk Collegiate in Norfolk, VA. He writes poetry in his spare time, which he has because he neglects other things. His poetry has been featured in *Silver Rose Magazine*, *Flying South*, and *Wild Roof Journal*.

Erin Birdsall is a writer living in Pittsburgh, Pennsylvania, and holds a B.A. in English (Creative Writing—Fiction) from Northwestern University. She is currently drafting her first novel and has written a few short stories over the years. If you read her work, you'll encounter stories about women, Celtic folklore, grief, magic, and spirituality.

Jack Bordnick's sculptural and photographic imagery is a reflection of his past and present forces as well as the imagination of his life's stories. They represent an evolutionary process of these ideas and how all of life's forces are interconnected, embraced and expressed through creative art forms. He calls it "my quantum and metaphoric moment, the changing from one form to another." They express and implement his thoughts and feelings regarding taking risks without any guarantee of their success.

Miriam Borgstrom resides in the neon desert of Southern Nevada. She is an advocate for ampersands, eyeglasses, and avocados. Borgstrom's most recent work can be found at *Monday Night* and *Dream Pop Press*. Find her online at www.amiareiaam.com.

Christopher Bowen is the author of the chapbook *We Were Giants*, the novella *When I Return to You, I Will Be Unfed*, and the nonfiction *Debt*. He was a semifinalist in the 2017 Faulkner-Wisdom Novella Competition and received honorable mention in the 45th New Millennium Writing Awards in the nonfiction category.

Christopher Paul Brown is known for his exploration of the unconscious through improvisation and the cultivation of serendipity and synchronicity via alchemy. His first photography sale was to the collection of the Standard Oil Company of Indiana, and his video, *You Define Single File*, was nominated for the Golden Gate Award in 2004. Over the past four years, his art was exhibited twice in Rome, Italy, in Belgrade, Serbia, and his series, *Obscure Reveal*, was exhibited at a Florida museum in 2017. His work appears in two hardcover books released by Manifest Gallery, and in *Tusis, Manipulated Images, a Dek Unu* (2019).

Tifara Brown was born and raised in the Deep South, and has been writing original poetry since 2013. She has shared her poetry on the TEDx stage and competed across the country in the art of spoken word. Her work appears in various magazines, and she published a book of poems entitled *Honeysuckle: Poems and Stories from a Black Southerner* in memory of her ancestor, a victim of racial violence. She is passionate about storytelling and uses her words as a vehicle for youth advocacy and the reduction of violence.

Tetman Callis was born in the Northeast and raised in the Southwest; his father a soldier and his mother a homemaker. His short fiction has appeared in *NOON*, *New York Tyrant*, *Best Microfiction 2019*, *Atticus Review*, and *Writing Disorder*. He is the author of the memoir *High Street: Lawyers, Guns & Money in a Stoner's New Mexico* (2012, Outpost 19), and the children's chapter book *Franny & Toby* (2015, Silky Oak Press). He lives in Chicago with his wife and their two cats, and makes his living as a paralegal.

Garrett Candrea grew up in Eastchester, New York and currently lives in Astoria, Queens. His work has appeared in *Sunspot.*

Steve Capra is a playwright and theater writer living in New York City. His plays have been produced in New York and the UK. His dramatic poem, *The Fall*, was a finalist in The Bordighera Poetry Prize Competition; his play, *The Shanghai Arsonist*, was a finalist in The Tennessee Williams Short Play Competition; his play, *At Night in Praha*, was a finalist in The American Globe Festival and placed third in The New Venture Festival. His book, *Theater Voices*, includes interviews with leaders in the British and American theater.

Martha Clarkson's writing and photography can be found in *F-Stop*, *Seattle Review*, *Portland Review*, *Black Box Gallery*, *Tulane Review*, *Seattle Times*, *Hawaii Pacific Review*, *Feminine Rising*, *Nimrod*, *Tipton Poetry Journal*, *Rattle*, and many more. *Her Voices, Her Room* won the short story prize from Open City/Anderbo. She has two notable short stories in *Best American Short Stories*. https://www.marthaclarkson.com

Meagan Daine is a multimedia storyteller specializing in alternative coming-of-age tales about diverse characters in extraordinary circumstances. Born and raised in East Texas, she moved away to attend the all-female Mills College in Oakland, CA. She worked as a waitress, an ESL teacher, a "jolly" in a Roman dance club, a theatre manager, a magician's assistant, and a private investigator while establishing her writing career. Her stage plays have been performed at various venues. Her first feature film, contemporary Western thriller *West of Redemption* (Kairos Productions, starring Billy Zane), won multiple festival awards. She is a staff writer on the one-hour television drama *Games People Play.*

After a nomadic, army-brat childhood, **Carolyn Dasher** found her true home in Portland, Oregon, where she lives with her husband and a cat who thinks it's a dog. When she's not writing, she's probably fixing something in her hundred-year-old house.

Leah Dockrill is a Toronto-based visual artist. Her practice includes painting and collage, both of which have been exhibited in Canada and the US. In recent years, her work has been published in over three dozen art and literature journals, including *Sunspot* (Spring 2019). She was the featured artist in *Mud Season*, *Beyond Words*, *Fauxmoir*, and *Gulf Stream*. Dockrill is an elected member of the Society of Canadian Artists, and the Colour and Form Society (Canada). Her work is represented by two Ontario galleries: Tag Art Gallery and NOWORDS.

Roopa Dudley loves to paint art that portrays chess in some fashion. She became a full-time painter after she got laid off unexpectedly from a job as a linguist, which she enjoyed and earned her a pretty penny. That gave Dudley an opportunity to start a new career based on what she really wanted to do but had never found the courage to pursue. She loves going to museums and reading about 20th century artists. She is married and lives with her two daughters in Severn, MD.

Bryan Edenfield is the author of *Cake*, published by Really Serious Literature. He was born and raised in Arizona, but has lived in Washington State since 2007. He has been alive for a few decades.

Laura Eppinger has had work nominated for a Pushcart Prize and Best of the Net. Her work has appeared at *The Rumpus*, *The Toast*, and elsewhere. Visit her here: https://lauraeppinger.blog/workspub/ She tweets at @lola_epp.

Oisin Farraige writes poetry and lives in SC.

Julie Esther Fisher's stories have appeared or are forthcoming in the *Alaska Quarterly*, *Chicago Quarterly*, *Prime Number*, *William and Mary Review*, *Other Voices*, and others, and is forthcoming in *Bridge Eight*. She has been a finalist in Boulevard's Short Fiction contest and in Arts and Letters Unclassifiables. A passionate gardener dedicated to sustainability, she lives on several hundred acres of conserved land in western Massachusetts.

Chris Fleming is a writer and translator from Sydney, Australia, whose fiction and nonfiction has appeared in scholarly and popular media, including *Westerly*, *Guardian*, *Sydney Review of Books*, *Saturday Paper*, *LA Review*, and *Chronicle Review*. He's the author or editor of ten books, most recently of *On Drugs* (Giramondo, 2019). He's currently Associate Professor in Humanities and a Member of the Writing and Society Research Centre at Western Sydney University, Australia.

In her writing, **Atma Frans** searches for the voice beneath her personas: woman, mother, trauma survivor, immigrant, architect, queer, poet. Her stories and poems have been longlisted for contests and are published in *New Quarterly*, *Arc Poetry*, *CV2*, *Chiron*, *Obsessed with Pipework*, *Lighthouse*, *Dalhousie*, and elsewhere. She lives in Gibsons, BC, Canada.

Bianca Giglio is a Canadian university student in the process of completing Bachelor's degrees in both Biology and Women's Studies.

Lindsey Morrison Grant is a self-identifying neurodivergent, two-spirit, elder storyteller, and contrarian deeply rooted in the roar and lore of what's become Portlandia of The Left Coast. The Artist attributes success and survival (if not salvation) to superlative supports, mindfulness practice, and daily creative expression in words, sounds, and images.

Phyllis Green is an author, playwright, and artist. Her art has appeared in *ArLiJo 123*, *Gulf Stream*, *Novus*, *New Plains*, *CERASUS*, *FERAL*, *Superpresent* and others, and is forthcoming in *CALYX Aji*, *Rip Rap*, *Inscape*, *Foreshadow*, *I 70 Reviand*, *Wild Roof*, and *Cinematic Codes*.

Valyntina Grenier is a multi-genre artist living with her wife in Tucson, AZ. She works with paint, ink, Neon, encaustic medium, recycled or repurposed materials, and words. She is the author of two poetry chapbooks, *Fever Dream/ Take Heart* (Cathexis Northwest Press 2020) and *In Our Now* (Finishing Line Press 2022). Her work appears in *Impermanent Earth*, *The Journal*, *Lana Turner*, and *The Night Heron Barks*. Find her at valyntinagrenier.com or Insta @valyntinagrenier.

Matt Gulley attended Wayne State University in Detroit and the MFA program at Long Island University in Brooklyn. He currently resides in Brooklyn with his girlfriend, Jenna, and tries to write a little bit every day.

HR Harper is a poet living in the redwoods above Santa Cruz, CA. In recent months he's had poems published in *Prospectus*, *The Write Launch*, a Wingless Dreamer anthology, *The Vital Sparks*, *The 34thParallel Magazine*, *High Shelf Press* journal, and *Angel Rust* magazine. A student/practitioner of Dzogchen meditation, he writes to understand, heal and resolve the curious limits and contradictions of consciousness in a world that is being destroyed by humans.

JJ Chen Henderson is a writer, poet, and artist. She has published a novel, short stories and poetry in venues such as *Fourteen Hills*, *Poetry East*, *Clackamas*, and *SLANT*.

Mark Henderson teaches English at Tuskegee University. He earned his Ph.D. at Auburn University with concentrations in American literature and psychoanalytic theory. He has poems published or forthcoming in *Cozy Cat Press*, *From Whispers to Roars*, Defenestrationism.net, *Bombfire*, *Former People*, *Neologism*, *Broad River Review*, *Rune Bear*, *Flora Fiction*, *Flare*, *Visitant*, *Blood Tree Literature*, *The Closed Eye Open*, *Last Stanza Poetry Journal*, *Burningword*, *Better Than Starbucks*, and *The Racket*. He was born and raised in Monroe, Louisiana, and currently resides in Auburn, Alabama.

Susanna Herrmann is a designer and visual artist from Bloomington, Indiana. She studied philosophy at Georgetown University before doing some photography and curation work and pursuing an MFA in studio art at the Eskenazi School of Art, Architecture, and Design at Indiana University. Susanna's work is based in theories of visual perception and is influenced by space and landscape. Themes of orientation and navigation are found throughout her work. She enjoys mixing analog and digital methods. Her current work centers experiences of landscapes.

DS Higdon is a writer from Kentucky. His work has been published or is forthcoming in *Rust + Moth, Exposition Review, Lucky Jefferson, Coffin Bell Journal*, and others. He is the 2021 winner of The Grand Prix Prize from the Kentucky State Poetry Society. He lives with his family in Louisville, KY.

Discharged from the Army in 1955, after being exposed to Asian art, **Larry Hill** discovered the renowned New York School of Painting. Seeing the work of Jackson Pollock, Franz Kline, and Willem de Kooning changed his life. Hill's work was displayed and sold with theirs at the Sidney Janis gallery in New York. According to Samsung, he is one of the top 100 living artists in the world. He gets up almost every day, walks to his garage/studio and tackle a painting, usually one over six feet. At an Ikebana Society show, the great William Saroyan left him a note describing his work as "heroic." https://www.larryhillartist-writer.com/

Irene Blair Honeycutt's fourth poetry book, *Beneath the Bamboo Sky* (Main Street Rag 2017), is subtitled *Poems and Pieces on Loss and Consolation* because "It is my attempt to honor life by giving voice to sorrow and joy. Much of the book is about the loss of siblings—a grief not often recognized in our culture." Irene founded Central Piedmont Community College's annual literary festival Sensoria. Her work has been published in *Nimrod, Southern Poetry, The Southern Poetry Anthology: VII*, and *Virginia Quarterly*. Garrison Keillor included one of her poems on *Writers Almanac.* Irene has studied in the Czech Republic, Ireland, and Iceland. She lives in Indian Trail, NC.

Rain Hou is a junior high-school student who majors in music but is also passionate about writing.

Meg Hurtado Bloom has her MFA in Poetry from St Mary's College of California. She also studied English and Art History at the University of Richmond. Meg's work has appeared in *The Volta, Cannibal, Hidden City Quarterly*, the *West Wind Review, POOL*, the *Columbia Poetry Review*, and the McSweeney's anthology *Conversations at the Wartime Cafe*. She has worked for VERSE, Wave Books, and Omnidawn.

Candice Kelsey teaches writing in the South. Her poetry appears in *Poets Reading the News* and *Poet Lore*, among other journals, and her first collection, *Still I am Pushing*, explores mother-daughter relationships as well as toxic body messages. She won the 2019 Two Sisters Writing's Contest and was recently nominated for both a Best of the Net and a Pushcart. Find her at www.candicemkelseypoet.com.

Sarah Kersey is a poet and graduate student in the MFA Creative Writing program at Eastern Washington. Her work has been published by *Write About Now, Awakenings Foundation*, and publications by Gonzaga University. Kersey lives in Spokane, Washington and work as the managing editor of *Willow Springs Books*.

Serge Lecomte was born in Belgium and spent his teens in South Philly and Brooklyn. He joined the Air Force Medical Corps and was sent to Selma, Alabama during the Civil Rights Movement. There he was a crew member on helicopter rescue. Lecomte received a B.A. in Russian Studies from the University of Alabama, and earned an M.A.

and Ph.D. from Vanderbilt University in Russian Literature with a minor in French Literature. Lecomte is also a published novelist, poet and playwright. For several years he was the poetry editor for *Paper Radio*. He recently moved to Bellingham, WA.

Naomi Ruth Lowinsky won the Atlanta Review International Merit Award, the Blue Light Poetry Prize, and the Obama Millennial Award. Her fourth full-length collection, *The Faust Woman Poems*, trace one woman's Faustian adventures through Women's Liberation and the return of the Goddess. Her new collection of poems, *Death and His Lorca*, was recently published by Blue Light Press. She is the poetry editor for *Psychological Perspectives* and blogs about poetry and life at sisterfrombelow.com.

Roeethyll Lunn is a lifelong educator, learner, and writer. For many years she has been a Developmental Writing Instructor at Wayne Community College in Goldsboro, NC. She declares herself to be "an experimental writer" of essays, short stories, poetry, and articles about people living in the Pee Dee area of rural South Carolina just before desegregation. She was born in Darlington, South Carolina, has a BFA in Broadcast Media and an MFA in English and writing.

Evelyn M is an interior designer, artist and micro urban flower farmer living in Campbell River. She was born in Vancouver where she received her Associate of Interior Design from Douglas College after which she continued her education studying building technology and art. Evelyn began a career in fine art with her detailed custom watercolors of dogs, cats and people, soon expanding to wildlife of the Antarctic. Evelyn M moved to the islands at 30 where the influences of the city and rural/suburban life became a strong part of her art and design. Recently, she has embraced digital photography. Her work can be found at www.EvelynM.com.

Ryan Mattern holds an MA in English from UC Davis, and a BA in Creative Writing from CSUSB. He is the recipient of the Felix Valdez Award. His work has appeared in *Crazyhorse*, *The Santa Clara Review*, and *Poetry Quarterly*. He currently serves in the US Army.

Tyler McCurry is a thirty-one-year-old author from Olathe, Kansas with a passion for food, family, and fun. His work has appeared in *Davega Bicycle*, *Aphelion Webzine*, the JCCC literary magazine *Mind's Eye*, the University of Kansas literary magazine *Coal City Review*, *Grand Little Thing*, *Fleas on the Dog* and *Clinch: A Martial Arts Literary Magazine*.

Paul Milligan is a research pharmacist who writes academic papers as his vocation, and poems and flash fiction as his avocation. He also dabbles in sculpture when the message requires. He is developing a daily writing habit but finding that difficult to meld with his daily Scotch habit.

Haylee Millikan is a poet originally from Spokane. Haylee's work focuses on themes of intimacy, disability, self, and the elusive concept of home, and has been featured in *Equinox*, *Litro*, *Beyond Words*, *Susie Magazine*, *Textploit*, *pioneertown*, and others. They currently reside in Long Beach with their two Flatbush rescue cats.

Martha Nance is a physician in Minnesota whose bored iPhone sometimes puts on its macro lens and takes pictures, which she then tries to translate into something a human can relate to. Her photographs have been published in *Tiny Seed, Fredericksburg Literary and Art Review, Raw Art Review,* and *Northwest Review,* among others.

Robert Palmer graduated Sum Cum Laude from ASU with a degree in Fine Art, Painting in 2003. Roberts' choice of medium is typically oil paint and watercolor. Some work has been contributed to organizations for charity. His work has been presented in several shows in Utah and Arizona.

A published poet, writer, and artist, **Jen Payne** is the author of several books including *LOOK UP! Musings on the Nature of Mindfulness, Evidence of Flossing: What We Leave Behind, Waiting Out the Storm,* and *Water Under the Bridge: A Sort-of Love Story.* She is the creator/editor of *MANIFEST* (zine), and writes regularly on her blog: www.randomactsofwriting.net.

Sunny Payson received an MFA in poetry, but has gravitated to fiction over the years. Payson lives in Vermont with family.

Michael Pearce's poetry has appeared in *The Threepenny Review, The Yale Review, Nimrod, Spillway, The Gettysburg Review, The Sun,* and elsewhere, and has won several national prizes (New Ohio Review, Oberon, Dogwood, and others). His collection of poems, *Santa Lucia by Starlight,* won the Brighthorse Prize and will be published in 2022.

LG Pomerleau is a writer of poetry and historical fiction, living in Nanton, Alberta, Canada. Pomerleau has written two novels and is a published poet, with poems currently in print in literary magazines and anthologies in Canada, the US, and abroad.

Karen Poppy has work published in numerous literary journals, magazines, and anthologies. Her chapbook *Crack Open/Emergency* was published by Finishing Line Press (2020), where she has another chapbook forthcoming. Her chapbook *Every Possible Thing* is published by Homestead Lighthouse Press (2020). An attorney licensed in California and Texas, Karen Poppy lives in the San Francisco Bay Area.

Ron Pullins is a fiction writer, playwright, and poet working in Tucson AZ. His works in fiction, poetry and drama have been published in numerous journals, including *Typishly, Southwest Review,* and *Shenandoah.*

K.G. Ricci is a self-taught NYC artist who has been creating collages for the past seven years. In that time, his work has evolved from the larger 24x48 panels to the current 7x10 books. His work has been in gallery exhibitions throughout the country, and he has appeared in numerous online exhibitions. Many of Ken's recent "visual stories" have been featured in literary magazines.

jessica ross is an editor, writer, and podcaster; they write and edit for tabletop roleplaying games like Scarred Lands, Starfinder, and Dungeons & Dragons, and they play TRPGs with the d20 Dames, a family-friendly actual play podcast. You can find all of their writing and other projects on their website: writejess.com.

Noah Ruiz was born in Michigan and raised in Colorado. He attended Colorado State University, where he was published for the first time in *Greyrock Review.* After studying English, history, rhetoric, linguistics, and literacy, he moved to Florida to pursue his writing and his music.

Federica Santini lives in Atlanta and teaches at Kennesaw State University. She holds an MA from the University of Siena, Italy, and a PhD from UCLA. She has authored or edited four volumes on poetics, and her poetry and fiction has been published in numerous journals in North America and Europe. She is the author of the poetry chapbook *Unearthed* (Kelsay Books, 2021).

Jacqueline Schaalje has published short fiction and poetry in *Massachusetts Review, Talking Writing, Frontier Poetry, Grist, Six Sentences*, and others. She has received scholarships at the Southampton Writers Conference and International Women's Writing Guild. She is a member of the Israel Association for Writers in English and the current editor of *arc.* She earned her MA in English from the University of Amsterdam.

Aarron Sholar is a transgender writer who has essays forthcoming and published in *Dead Skunk Magazine, Broadkill Review, Beaver Magazine, Sierra Nevada Review, 45th Parallel Literary Magazine, Hobart, Polaris Magazine*, and others. He holds a BA from Salisbury University and is an MFA candidate in CNF at MNSU, Mankato, where he is Head CNF Editor of *Blue Earth Review.*

Jacqueline Shortell-McSweeney writes only when inspired, or when her muse Noreen stands over her with a metaphorical rolling pin. At other times, she has worked as a producer for Women Make Movies, a video artist at Henry St., Settlement, first union woman grip, and then as a lawyer, in the hopes that she could sue for some of her Me-too moments. Now retired to her writing desk, Shortell-McSweeney has been published in eight anthologies, the latest being *Beat Generation. Dr. Altman and the Concubines* is available in bookstores. Most important, she spends precious time with her loving family.

Murray Silverstein has been published in *RATTLE, Brief Wilderness, Brooklyn Review, Cape Rock Poetry, Euphony, Spillway, Poetry East, West Marin Review, RUNES, Nimrod, Connecticut Review, Hollins Critic, ZYZZYVA, California Quarterly, El Portal, Elysian Fields, Fourteen Hills, Front Range, Louisiana Literature, The MacGuffin, The Meadow*, and *Pembroke Magazine*, among others. His two books of poetry are *Master of Leaves* (2014) and *Any Old Wolf* (2007). Silverstein is the senior editor of *America, We Call Your Name* (2018). A retired architect, Silverstein holds a master's in architecture.

A retired educator, **Dave Sims** makes art and music in the mountains of central Pennsylvania. Since 2016, his paintings and comix, both old-school and digital, have appeared in dozens of tactile and virtual exhibits and publications. Recent work is available or forthcoming in *Fauxmoir Review, Peatsmoke, Beyond Words*, and *Inverted*

Syntax. He just finished a new song for another beautiful grandchild named Waylon James, who was born on June 18th, 2022. Experience more at www.tincansims.com.

Professor Emeritus of English at Ohio Northern University **Claude Clayton Smith** is the author of eight books and coeditor/translator of four others. His own work has been translated into five languages, including Russian and Chinese. For further information visit: claudeclaytonsmith.wordpress.com.

Kate Strong Stadt is a former children's librarian turned knowledge worker. Recently, her poems have been published in *The Collidescope*, *Sparked Literary Magazine*, and *swifts & slows*. Her latest obsession is blacksmithing.

Alex Stanley is a graduate of Boston College, and he received his MFA in Creative Writing at the University of California, Irvine. He is a former sports journalist, and his sports writing has been featured in *Sports Illustrated*. His published poems have appeared in *American Poets Magazine*, *HCE Review*, *Helix Magazine*, *Duck Lake Journal*, *The Write Launch*, and *Doozine*. He is a recipient of the 2021 Academy of American Poets Award. He resides in Costa Mesa, CA.

Travis Stephens is a tugboat captain who resides with his family in California. An alumni of the University of Wisconsin-Eau Claire, recent credits include: *2River*, *Sheila-Na-Gig*, *Hole in the Head Review*, *Griffel*, and *The Dead Mule School of Southern Literature*. Visit him at: zolothstephenswrites.com.

Jack Stewart was educated at the University of Alabama and Emory University. From 1992 to 1995 he was a Brittain Fellow at The Georgia Institute of Technology. His first book, *No Reason*, was published by the Poeima Poetry Series in 2020, and his work has appeared in numerous journals and anthologies, including *Poetry*, *American Literary Review*, *Nimrod*, and *Image*.

Joanna Urban's writing has appeared in *Belle Ombre*, *District Lit*, *Yoga Digest*, and other publications.

Janna Urschel has been a wedding harpist, dog musher, native language linguist, children's Spanish teacher, and college writing instructor. She is currently a PhD student in English at SUNY. Janna recently relocated to the high plains of Wyoming, where she is at work on a creative dissertation exploring nonhuman agency. She has been published in *Trolley*, *Mamalode*, and *Ladybug*. She was a finalist for the 2021 Montana Prize, and blogs at www.lifeinthemultiverse.com.

Jose Varghese is the author of *Silver Painted Gandhi and Other Poems*, and his short story manuscript *In/Sane* was a finalist in the 2018 Beverly International Prize. His second collection of poems is scheduled for publication in 2022 by Black Spring Press Group, UK. He was a finalist twice in the London Independent Story Prize (LISP), a runner up in the Salt Prize, and was commended in the Gregory O'Donoghue International Poetry Prize. His works are published or forthcoming in a number of journals and magazines.

Sally Ventura lives and teaches in Olean, New York. She has published poems and essays in *Blue Collar Review, A Plate of Pandemic, English Journal, English Record, Sisyphus, Teachers and Writers Collaborative, College English Association Critic, Earth's Daughters,* and *Midwest Quarterly.*

Pamela Viggiani is a mixed-media artist and art educator living in Canandaigua, NY. A native of the Finger Lakes region, she began teaching art in 1986. Her work has been featured in *Small Works, Light Space & Time, Another Chicago Magazine, Press Pause Press, From Whispers to Roars, Sunspot,* and *Beyond Words.* In a converted fruit cellar, Pamela produces abstract visual interpretations of particular concepts to explore the relationship between word and meaning. Her small works are often manifestations of ambiguity, allowing for varied reactions. Some works, however, reflect the world back to the viewer with more clarity, revealing hidden realities and challenging entrenched ways of thinking.

Adam Walsh's poetry has appeared in *the Journal, Hawaii Review, Crab Creek, Istanbul Review, Barrow Street,* and *BLAZEVox,* among others. His chapbook *metabody* was a finalist at the Atlas Review. He lives in Micronesia and works as an instructor in the Languages and Humanities Department at Northern Marianas College.

Jeanne Wilkinson is a writer and artist sharing time between Brooklyn, NY and Madison, WI. From being a "back-to-the-land" organic dairy farmer in Wisconsin, she ended up with an MFA in painting at Pratt Institute. Her essays have been featured on WNYC's Leonard Lopate Show and NPR's *Living on Earth.* Her fiction has appeared in *Columbia Journal* and *Digging Through the Fat,* and chapters from her memoir *1969: My Year with a San Francisco Drug Dealer,* have been published by *Raven's Perch, New Millennium Writings,* and more. See her website at https://jeannewilkinson.com.

Mikal Wix grew up in the American South, which seeded insights into many outlooks, including visions of a revenant from the closet. He has work in or forthcoming in *Corvus, Jupiter Review, Berkeley Poetry, Tahoma Literary, Hyacinth, Roi Fainéant Press, Fiery Scribe,* and others. He works as a science editor.

Cynthia Yatchman is a Seattle based artist and art instructor. With an M.A. in child development and a B.A. in education, she has a strong interest in art education and teaches art to adults, children, and families. As a former ceramicist, she studied with J.T. Abernathy in Ann Arbor, MI. After receiving her B.F.A. in painting from the University of Washington, she switched from 3D art to 2D. She works primarily on paintings, prints and collages. Her art is housed in numerous public and private collections, and she has shown nationally. She is a member of the Seattle Print Art Association and COCA (Center of Contemporary Art).

WRITING A NEW WORLD

Sunspot Literary Journal believes in the power of the written word. Fiction, nonfiction, poetry and art can speak truth to power with the power inherent in all human beings. Our mission is to amplify every voice. Four digital quarterly editions are produced per year, along with one print volume.

SUPPORT *SUNSPOT LIT*

Today more than ever, literary journals are forces of change in the world. *Sunspot Lit* is funded entirely through private means. Every donation, even ones as small as a dollar, makes a difference. Please take a moment to drop a few bucks into the *Sunspot* magnetic field flux.

A PayPal link on the website makes it easy to send a tip, donate enough to publish the next digital edition, or go supernova and fund the next print edition. Please visit https://sunspotlit.com/support for details.

ADVERTISE IN *SUNSPOT*

Classified ads are available in quarterly digital editions and special editions. Spread the word about your writing and arts contests, residency programs, awards, workshops, and more. All classified ads are also posted on the website's classified page. Ad rate: $150 for up to 25 words; $5 for each additional word.

Print ads are available for the annual edition. All ads are black and white. A full page is $850, a half page is $450, and a quarter page is $295. Buy two ads of the same size for the same issue or for two sequential issues to receive a 10% discount. Set up three or more ads and receive a 15% discount.

Sunspot's groovy graphic designer can set up your ad to your specifications. Flat rate of $325, and the design is yours to use multiple times in *Sunspot* or any other magazine.

Sunspot Literary Journal

Writing a New World

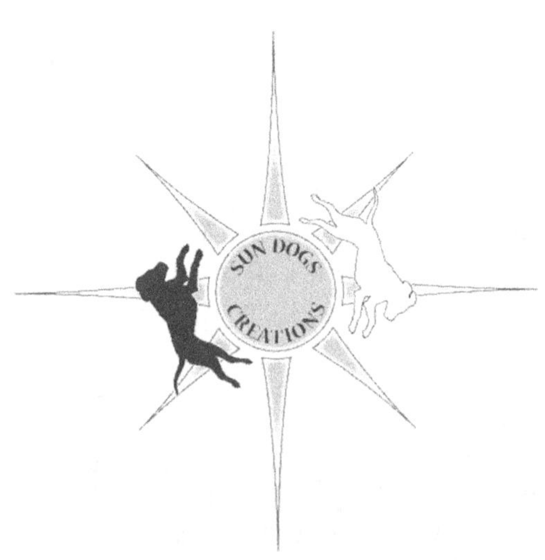

Sun Dogs Creations

Changing the World One Book at a Time